Johann
Sebastian
Bach

Play by Play

Johann Sebastian Bach

Play by Play

by
Alan Rich

with performances by
The Bach Ensemble,
Joshua Rifkin, conductor

A Newport Classic CD/B™
Presentation

HarperCollinsSanFrancisco,
1995

Credits

Executive Producer for the Series: *Lawrence J. Kraman*

Series Editor: *Jackson Braider*

Analytical Indexing: *John Ostendorf, Rudolph Palmer, Christopher Woltman*

Art Director: *Ann E. Kook*

Interior Design: *Stuart L. Silberman*

This recording was originally released on the L'Oiseau-Lyre label, # 417 250-2.

Library of Congress Cataloging-in-Publication Data

Rich, Alan.
  Johann Sebastian Bach : play by play / by Alan Rich ; with
performances by the Bach Ensemble, Joshua Rifkin, conductor.
    p. cm.
  "A Newport Classic CD/B presentation."
  Discography:
  Includes bibliographical references (p. 157).
  ISBN 0-06-263547-6
  ISBN 0-06-263550-6
  1. Bach, Johann Sebastian, 1685-1750. 2. Bach, Johann Sebastian,
1685-1750. *Herz und Mund und Tat und Leben.* (Cantata) 3. Bach, Johann
Sebastian, 1685-1750. *Ein Feste Burg ist unser Gott* (Cantata). 4. Music
appreciation.

ML410.B1R43 1995   94-49113
780' .92—dc20   CIP
                                                                  MN

        95 96 97 98 99 ❖ RRD(C) 10 9 8 7 6 5 4 3 2 1

Contents

A Note from the Executive Producer

o

IT IS NOT WITHOUT SOME IRONY that we have chosen to call the *Play by Play* series a "CD/B" presentation. Where the race is on in computer circles to define the *next* multimedia delivery system—though the various parties involved have never actually agreed as to what the current one is—we have concocted this marriage between two very different media, invented at least one millennium and half-a-world apart. It is, as you can see, very much a *low-tech* affair: a book and a compact disc.

Mind you, we have always been very conscious of the fact that this is a new medium. It isn't just a book with a CD pasted into it for fun, nor it is a CD with a hefty set of liner notes. Each illuminates the other; each brings something to the other what it might otherwise lack, particularly as regards the exploration, the appreciation, the *understanding* of music.

I feel a bit like Cecil B. DeMille in all of this: yes, the CD/B has been ten years in the making, but the cast has certainly not been in the thousands. Clayton Carlson and Bill Crowley, of HarperCollins and PolyGram respectively, caught on very quickly, and without their enthusiastic support, it is fair to say that none of this would have happened. The people in both their organizations—James McAndrew, Leslie Clagett, Justine Davis—have all been absolutely wonderful to work with.

Somewhere along the way, classical music became *serious* music, and when that happened, many of us lost touch with the idea that this music—heavy and heady as it can be sometimes—was very often supposed to be delightful, a pleasure, a source of enlightenment. I hope that this series will open up for you what has been, up to this point, a very closed world.

LAWRENCE J. KRAMAN

Author's Note

o

As an undergraduate at Harvard, slogging my way through a pre-med major but with my heart in the Music Department, I learned to think about the listening experience as an ongoing narrative, full of thrills and surprises. The wonderful G. Wallace Woodworth would start a Haydn symphony on the 78-rpm record player, then pick up the tone arm and make us guess what was going to happen next. (We were usually wrong, but that wasn't the point.) I learned about the momentum of Beethoven's Ninth Symphony from Donald Tovey's measure-by-measure "précis" in the first volume of his *Essays in Musical Analysis* (omitted, for reasons not fathomable, in the current reprint edition of these essential musical insights). Woody in the classroom, and Tovey on paper, have shaped the way I think about listening to music over half a century. Now, however, I don't have to dash to the piano to play Tovey's musical squibs; I can hand them off, second-by-second or CD index-by-index, as clearly as if Woody were still up front running the Victrola. You can, too; that's what *Play by Play* will do for you, for me, and for music.

ALAN RICH,
LOS ANGELES, 1995

How to Use
This Book

o

THE CD included with this volume has been analytically indexed.
That is to say, within each track on the compact disc there has
been embedded a series of inaudible codes that allows the listener
to access particular moments in the composition, be it something
as quick as the entry of the bass part in a fugue or something as
fundamental as the start of the recapitulation section in a sonata.

The various CD player manufacturers all have developed
their own particular way of accessing the index points on a compact disc and the reader should consult his or her manual for the
appropriate instructions. Some older models of machines have
no such capacity. However, the trick in using the sections of this
book devoted to Analytical Indexing—the Play by Play section
and the Essential Recordings section immediately following it—
is to look at the tracking display on the CD player and relate it to
what you are reading about in the book.

Here is a typical example of what will appear in the text: [T2/i3, 1:29]. This provides the reader three pieces of information: the track (T2), the index point (i3), and the absolute time of the event in the track (1:29). What this shorthand describes, then, is third index point on the second track of the compact disc, which occurs at 1:29 into the track. So, even if your CD player doesn't have indexing, the time display will give you a precise indication of the moment a particular event being described in the text will occur.

The Rise of
the Baroque

o

LIKE MANY MOVEMENTS in the history of the arts, Baroque music
was born out of protest, launched by enthusiastic if not always
skilled amateurs. One may trace Johann Sebastian Bach's family
ancestry back through generations of musicians and merchants,
but Bach's *musical* ancestry—a large part of it, at any rate—hails
back to a gathering of dilettantes and parlor intellectuals in a
Florentine palace roughly a century before the composer's birth.
But while examining the roots of a musical tradition can answer
any number of historical questions, only the music can reveal its
special genius.

Some of the brightest intellectuals of the day gathered at the
home of Count Giovanni de' Bardi, a Florentine noble, a
Renaissance man, an earnest student of the arts, and a dilettante
in the best sense (from the same root as "delight"). These poets,
philosophers, artists, and perhaps a musician or two talked about

the state of the world, their discourse undoubtedly fueled by hearty Tuscan wine. One matter came under frequent and especially fervent discussion: how to save the art of music—which, the Bardi salon unanimously decided, had gone to the dogs. In 1581, the group produced *The Dialogue Between Ancient and Modern Music*, a belligerent essay written by member and composer Vincenzo Galilei (father of astronomer Galileo), which forcefully declared the music of the time in all ways corrupt. How did they propose to salvage the art? By returning to the practices of the ancient Greeks.

Apparently it didn't matter all that much to the "Camerata," as this Florentine gathering called itself, that nobody in sixteenth-century Italy had the vaguest notion of what ancient Greek music actually sounded like, much less how it was performed or by whom it was created. The few surviving scraps of manuscript could hardly be deciphered. They did know, however, that actors in Athenian classic drama chanted rather than spoke their lines, drawing upon various musical techniques to accentuate verbal passions.

The Florentine scholars envied music's distant past, as the music of their time consisted of the intricate church polyphony of Giovanni Pierluigi da Palestrina and the sensuous madrigals of Luca Marenzio and his colleagues. They felt that music had lost the power to express the human passions fundamental to all great art. The intricate contrapuntal textures of sacred and secular sixteenth-century music—in which a soprano in a love song might declaim one line of text while the tenor sang something else entirely—made it impossible, the Camerata wanted it known, to hear the words or to match the musical depiction of specific words with specific emotions.

In the place of this complexity, which in the Renaissance represented a high level of sophistication, the Florentines proposed simpler but more emotionally direct music, with one clearly audible singer supported by a few instruments. A new vocabulary of rich, lush harmonies would implement the emotional impact of the words, while poignant dissonances emphasized moments of sorrow or anguish. These Baroque pioneers couldn't have foreseen that this newly proclaimed simplicity would evolve once again, not many generations later, in music of astonishing and wondrous complexity—the grandiloquent, oratorical intricacy of a Bach **cantata** or a Handel **oratorio**. But music history often works that way.

Thus the music of the Baroque era, whose later works were prized for their grandeur and complexity, originated around 1600 in a return to the simplicity of an imagined past.

Claudio Monteverdi (1567-1643), the composer who transformed the theories of La Camerata into powerful, emotional musical expression.

Music at the start of the Baroque era typically called for an expressive solo with a dramatically passionate text sung to a chaste, unobtrusive accompaniment—a **keyboard instrument** perhaps supported by a small group of strings. The very word "Baroque," from an obscure Portuguese term, defined a kind of artwork that was irregularly shaped and, therefore, somewhat frantic. (Historians applied the term to this new music in retrospect.)

Composers such as Jacopo Peri and Giulio Caccini—whose names live on in history books if nowhere else—wrote entire **operas** in this new style. Their musical dramas told the familiar stories of classic mythology, one favorite being the tale of Orpheus, who tamed the guards of Hades with the power of his music to gain the release of his beloved Eurydice. Expressive as some moments in these works surely are, they were nonetheless limited by their composers' self-imposed austerities. The first ventures in *musica moderna* (one of several names coined for this newfangled music) strike ears today as pretty dull stuff.

One genius of the early Baroque, however, had the vision to seize upon these musical ideals and make them work. Claudio Monteverdi's 1607 *Orfeo* found a meeting-ground between the new, expressive song style and the more artistically balanced ideals of the very music his Florentine contemporaries hoped to banish. Alongside the soloists' passionate declamations, which carried the action forward, Monteverdi introduced choruses in the style of the old-fashioned madrigals, providing the variety in dramatic pacing and musical style early operas had lacked.

Monteverdi, then, first proclaimed the potential in the art of opera, and gave it the dramatic resonance to charm and arouse its audiences. Only three of his music dramas survive, but in all three one cannot help but be struck by the sureness with which the music matches the characters' thoughts: the yearning of the faithful Penelope awaiting the return of her long-absent Ulysses, the savagery of the evil Nero killing off his political enemies.

Opera took hold with the Italian public; and by 1650, most Northern Italian cities boasted public opera theaters. Audiences flocked in to cheer the vocal acrobatics of their favorite performers and to marvel at the incredible stage sets. Composers turned out grand operatic showpieces to enable virtuosos to show off their tonsils and their controlled breathing. Composers from the north— among them Germany's Heinrich Schütz and England's Henry Purcell—came to study how the Italians expressed deep human passions through the beauty of the melodic line.

Sensing a new market, Italian composers journeyed north to establish their style of music in other lands. Most notable among these was the clever and opportunistic Florentine Giovanni Battista Lulli, a conniving character who went to Paris in the middle of the seventeenth century, changed his name to Jean-Baptiste Lully, and established himself as music master at the court of King Louis XIV in Versailles.

The rise of Italian opera throughout the seventeenth century proclaimed the gorgeous voice singing the gorgeous melody as the supreme triumph of the art of music. But late in the century, a similar phenomenon emerged in the realm of instrumental music when a group—again, mostly in Italy—set out to create a family of string instruments whose sweet but wordless singing could stand as a counterpart to the passions of opera. A generation of master builders—Antonio Stradivari, as well as the Amatis and the Guarneris—redesigned the then-common family of viols into the violin, viola, and cello of modern usage, sweeter in tone and more conducive to feats of virtuosity.

The new instrumental music created a taste for string music that rivaled the passion for virtuosic operatic singing. Composers took up writing for the string instruments with the same alacrity others had brought to opera. Arcangelo Corelli virtually invented the new instrumental forms: the **sonata,** for a solo instrument supported by keyboard; the **trio sonata,** for an intertwined group of three soloists plus the supporting keyboard (both forms clear relatives of the **arias** and duets in opera), and the **concerto grosso,** which builds on the differences between small and large groups of instruments—sometimes echoing one another and sometimes "contradicting" each other with contrasting melodies. Corelli's successors, most notably the fabulously prolific Antonio Vivaldi, spread the fame of the Italian orchestral music through their travels and published works; by 1720,

The Baroque Noise

Noise characterized the public square of the typical seventeenth-century German village, where the practice of hiring town musicians to perform outdoors—usually from atop a tower or steeple to guarantee maximum effectiveness—can be traced to medieval times. The Germans favored brass or wind instruments, which the musicians played to mark important public events or just to signal the hours. In Richard Wagner's *Die Meistersinger,* set in medieval Nürnberg, a night watchman wanders through the scene from time to time, sounding his horn to encourage people to praise God for a moment and then toddle off to bed.

By the seventeenth century, municipal brass choirs (*Stadtpfeifer* or *Turmbläser*) had become fixtures of the German cityscape.

Composers such as Johann Pezel produced extended suites of music for these ensembles, and their repertory also included harmonizations (either written out or improvised) of the Lutheran chorale for the particular day.

The passion for brassiness reached Bach through natural pathways: his father, Johann Ambrosius, served as the *Stadtpfeifer* at Eisenach. Throughout his career, Johann Sebastian delighted in letting loose the Baroque "Big Noise." The joyous peals of trumpets in the third and fourth Orchestral Suites from his time at Anhalt-Cöthen, and such Leipzig products as the Gloria from the *B-minor Mass,* the *Christmas Oratorio,* and the *Magnificat* suggest that whenever the occasion called for a larger-than-life musical treatment, and the requisite instruments were at hand, Bach put them to full use.

it was the rare palace on the European continent that didn't employ an **orchestra** adept in performing the latest sonata or **concerto** just in from the south, with an Italian *maestro di musica* up front.

Who heard all this new music? And where?

In 1637, serious music went public for the first time in history. That year saw the opening of San Casiano in Venice, the first auditorium accessible to anyone who could afford the price of a ticket. Until then, most music had been a private matter, presented in the palaces of nobles and wealthy merchants to entertain guests. Every town with any cultural pretensions now had its own public opera house, sometimes three or four, all ruled by strutting prima donnas (of every sex and inclination) and their fickle, vociferous fans. When religious authorities forbade the staging of operas—during Lent, for example—the oratorio became the entertainment of choice: high drama, usually based on a religious text, presented without staging but as musically lavish as any opera.

By the end of the seventeenth century, Italy had been utterly conquered by music. New religious music even began to sound like opera—and, in doing so, reached an audience that might have scorned the austere church fare of a century before.

To the north, however, the new music encountered resistance, not so much in the Catholic precincts of Austria and southern Germany but in the regions where the Protestantism of Martin Luther and the forces of Reformation held sway. Luther, himself a composer, saw to it that his Protestant congregations were lavishly surrounded with music at all church occasions. But the frivolity of the operatic style, with its prizing of individual virtuosity and fanciful plotting, found no place in the Lutheran scheme of things.

The Lutheran service took many of its musical forms—as well as a few tunes—from Catholic models. Luther's body of **chorale** melodies, derived mostly from traditional folk song, was the Evangelical (i.e., Lutheran) counterpart of the repertory of ancient Gregorian chant allotted to each day in the Catholic church year. Like

The Organ

As early as the third century B.C., public spaces in the Greco-Roman world sported instruments propelled by water and controlled by a player pulling on spring-loaded slides; these organs, which transmitted wind pressure to a set of pipes, were used for ceremonies, and ended up in the hands (and homes) of rulers and aristocrats alike. By the sixth century A.D., a bellows arrangement had replaced the water system, at which point the organ grew in size, noise potential, and popularity. Legend has it that the ruler of Constantinople presented Charlemagne, the first Emperor of the Holy Roman Empire, with an organ in 812.

The organ first appeared in Christian churches around that same time, and continued to proliferate throughout the Middle Ages; in 1619, composer Michael Praetorius admiringly described the fourteenth-century organ at Halberstadt, which seemed to have most of the features—several ranks of pipes, a footboard for playing the bass notes, and so on—of the instruments Bach would have known in his own day.

the contrapuntal masters who flourished in the churches of Italy and Austria, the Lutheran church composers fashioned elaborate compositions from these chorales. The main difference: Protestants insisted that everything be sung in the language of its people—in German or, across the Channel, in English.

Unlike their Italian counterparts, musicians of the early Baroque Protestant churches made no effort to renounce their descent from the contrapuntal masters of the Renaissance. The Lutheran organist devised contrapuntal compositions into which the

The history of the organ, then, is one of constant expansion: of separate stops to enhance the range of timbre, mechanisms to control volume, more sophisticated ways of maintaining air pressure. But the splendor of the organ gave it a social function as well: the more affluent churches in seventeenth-century France, England, Germany, Italy, and Spain proclaimed their wealth by installing several organs on different levels inside the buildings to create echo effects that anticipated what is now known as "stereo."

As a skilled and renowned organist, Bach frequently tested and commented on instruments around the country. *The Bach Reader,* a wonderful documentary history of Bach, offers dozens of memos complaining about instruments he encountered, and pinpointing what needed to be done to restore them to playable condition. Some of the writings make amusing reading, even to nonorganists— witness his warnings about making keys so narrow fingers could get stuck between them or pedals so far apart as to expose a player to possible rupture.

chorales of the new church often were woven. One counterpoint that played an important role in the development of musical styles up to their glorious culmination in the time of Bach: the tightly controlled, intricate **fugue** (known as *fuga* in Italian and *Fuge* in German).

The new vernacular church service, especially in the hands of late Baroque masters such as Bach and Dietrich Buxtehude, suggested a personal relationship between the worshiper and God that had apparently not interested proponents of the old Latin service. This emotional closeness obviously stirred Bach's imagination; it comes out in the miraculous conversational moments in his cantatas: the earthly being in dialogue with the Heavenly Spirit in the language of a love duet.

During his tenure as concertmaster at the court of Weimar, the young Bach came across some of the new Italian music, and found himself enchanted. The typical composer's way of expressing delight with somebody else's music, in the early eighteenth century, was to take the original work, walk around inside it (so to speak) to study its own individuality, then transcribe it for some other scoring. For instance, Bach might take a Vivaldi concerto for three violins and convert it into a work for three harpsichords, or fashion a concerto originally written for strings and arrange it for **organ.**

Many streams of artistic thought—only lightly touched upon here—converge in the music of this serious, scholarly genius whom the world will never totally comprehend. He never fully lost his

Northern provincialism, yet he allowed his thoughts to be infiltrated and his creative energies motivated by the exuberant melodic richness from the south. He is considered one of music's great teachers, yet almost nothing is known about his own educational background. Perhaps he didn't need any; the very universality of Bach's vision, in fact, is all it takes to appreciate his unique place in the creative world.

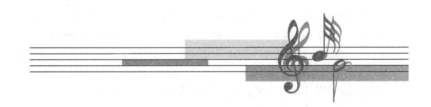

CHAPTER 2

Enter Bach

THE EARLIEST FIRM KNOWLEDGE of the Bach family centers around the modest figure of Veit Bach, a bread baker born in the mid-sixteenth century in the town of Wechmar. Veit (possibly Vitus) moved for a time to Hungary but returned to the German province of Thuringia in the face of growing Hungarian hostility toward Lutheranism. "Simple old Veit," as a genealogy compiled by his great-great-grandson Johann Sebastian refers to him, owned a cittern (a guitarlike instrument played with a pick), which he delighted in playing at his flour mill even as the wheels turned. "And this was, as it were," continues the genealogy, "the beginning of a musical inclination in his descendants."

Musical talent infused virtually every descendant of Veit Bach: his son Hans, also a baker as well as a town musician; another son Friedrich, who sent *his* three sons to Italy to further their musical education (though apparently without significant result); Christoph, son of Hans, a court musician at Weimar; Johann Ambrosius, one of Christoph's twin sons ("so much alike even their wives couldn't tell them apart," reads the genealogy), a *Stadtpfeifer* at Eisenach and the father of Johann Sebastian.

The Saxon town of Eisenach, birthplace not only of Bach but of Martin Luther, is not particularly striking. The ancient castle known as the Wartburg, the scene of the song contest in Richard Wagner's *Tannhäuser*, looms on a nearby crag. Johann Ambrosius found employment there as court and town musician, and then married Elisabeth Lämmerhirt, daughter of a furrier who was also a member of the Noble Council at nearby Erfurt. Of their eight children, four died young. Elisabeth gave birth to Johann Sebastian, the youngest son, on 21 March 1685, and had him baptized two days later.

Two of Bach's forebears: Hans Bach (c1555-1615) and Johann Ambrosius Bach (1643-1695). Hans was a carpenter by trade, though he was also the minstrel and "fool" at the court of Ursula, Duchess of Württemberg. Ambrosius, J.S. Bach's father, was well enough thought of by the Town Council of Eisenach to have his portrait painted. On the other hand, after he died, this same council refused to provide any support for his widow and children.

Hans Bach   **Johann Ambrosius Bach**

Sebastian's mother died in 1693, and his father shortly there-
after (although not before remarrying). The town council, however,
refused to support the new widow's family, which eventually scat-
tered: Sebastian and his brother Jacob went to their elder brother
Johann Christoph, organist at Ohrdruf and, according to Sebastian,
"a profound composer."

Although school records at Eisenach portray Sebastian as an
indifferent student with a singularly poor attendance record, his
father did succeed in training
him in the rudiments of

Bach's presumed birthplace in Eisenach.

music, most likely in playing string instruments. It was Christoph, however, a student of renowned organist and composer Johann Pachelbel, who gave Sebastian his first real musical training (in both keyboard playing and organ repair). And Sebastian gleaned his first awareness of the musical world outside the German provinces largely by copying Christoph's collection of manuscripts. By 1700, he attended St. Michael Academy at Lüneburg, where he earned high grades for his singing and his ability to improvise fugues at the keyboard. He also visited Hamburg, where he first came under the spell of world-class organists playing state-of-the-art instruments.

The early stages of Bach's professional career varied little from the lives of hundreds of musicians of the time: trudging from one audition to another, working as choirmaster, organist, or musical what-have-you at some provincial court or municipality, sustained by the hope that the treadmill might lead to a noble with a taste and appreciation for serious music or to a town with deep pockets and an enlightened council.

In this journey, Bach fared no better than most. In 1702, at 17, he failed an audition for an organist's post at Sangerhausen, then spent a year as lackey and violinist at the court at Weimar. A year later he landed an organist's job at Arnstadt, where he remained for four years despite tangles with church authorities over unauthorized absences, brawling with students, and inviting a "strange maiden" into his organ loft and (horror!) allowing her to play the instrument.

Musician Wanted: Must Be Versatile

Germany during the Baroque era saw little division between the "composer" and the "musician." Most players worth their salt were expected to decorate music on the spot through the addition of trills and other embellishments; others, like Bach, had to provide *and* perform works on a regular basis—along with polishing the silver, making the beds, or cutting the lawn, depending on their rank among the other servants in the palace. The real difference be-tween musicians was to be found in their titles; Bach, in the course of his working life, had no fewer than five titles. Here are his job descriptions:

◇ Violinist at the Court of Celle (1702): Play music in an ensemble under the direction of the Capellmeister. Obey elders and re-move the slop from the kitchen every morning.

◇ Organist at the Neukirche, Arnstadt (1703-7): Accompany the congregation in singing hymns from the second edition of the *Wittenberg Gesängbuch*. Teach the choir in the rendering of the chorales. Provide appropriate music for prelude and postlude of religious service, and do not play for too long or too short a time. Bear oneself as an abiding servant of God and the Town Consistory, and remember, *No Girls in the Organ Loft!*

◇ Concertmeister and Organist for Duke Wilhelm Ernst at the Court of

The New Church, Arnstadt: Bach began his working life here at the age of 18.

Prinz Johann Ernst von Wiemar: An early supporter of Bach and his music, Johann Ernst was responsible for getting Bach the job at Duke Wilhelm's palace in Weimar. Bach reciprocated by transcribing several of Johann Ernst's string concertos for organ.

Weimar (1708-17): Arrange music salubrious to acts of devotion to God for both organ and ensemble consisting of no less than eight strings, seven winds (including trumpets), and a kettledrum, plus a chorus of ten (four soloists). Obey all orders from your Master, Duke Wilhelm Ernst, and his surrogate, Capellmeister Salomo Drese. Act in the manner befitting an honor-loving servant of God and your Duke.

✧ Capellmeister for Prince Leopold at the Court of Anhalt-Cöthen (1718-23): Arrange and superintend music for all occasions in the court, including visits and celebrations of state. Maintain all the keyboard instruments and provide music for a mixed ensemble of strings and winds; when circumstances demand, you may add instrumentalists. Ask the Castle Steward for paper and ink to prepare scores and individual parts. Housing, candles, wood, wine, and a salary will be provided.

✧ Cantor of the Thomasschule and Music Director of the City of Leipzig (1723-50): Teach the boys Latin and singing and treat them in a courteous manner. Walk with them at all times, especially at funerals. Set for them a shining example of sobriety and honor. Arrange music for civic ceremonies and the city's four main churches so as to incite the listeners to devotion. Avoid creating an operatic impression.

The palace chapel at Weimar: this is the place where Bach composed and performed many of his most celebrated organ works, including the Toccata and Fugue in D minor.

The "strange maiden" was most likely Sebastian's cousin, Maria Barbara Bach, who he married in 1707. They had seven children, two of whom—Wilhelm Friedemann and Carl Philipp Emanuel—became composers in their own right. Bach's travels, meanwhile, took him to a four-month stint at the Parish of St. Blasius at Mühlhausen, thence to the court of Duke Wilhelm Ernst back at Weimar, where he remained for nine stormy but immensely productive years.

The Weimar court was rich and well-endowed, with a splendid organ and a small but well-paid orchestra and vocal ensemble. The Duke was fond of music, especially organ pieces, and he and his new organist/conductor/composer began life together in blissful harmony. For Bach, the post at Weimar allowed a measure of creative freedom that only musicians of his own time could have enjoyed—the chance to write and perform his music under the care of a more-or-less benevolent patron. He knew about the prominent musicians of the preceding generation—Dietrich Buxtehude with his mastery of the great organ at Lübeck, Johann Pachelbel at Nürnberg—and their vast organ works. Now he could try to surpass these role models. One measure of Bach's success is the celebrated *Toccata and Fugue in D Minor,* which probably dates from his early Weimar days, familiar from its inflationary treatment in Walt Disney's *Fantasia* but more remarkable for its sense of stretching toward something new on the horizon.

Weimar served as the window to a wider world than the young Bach had previously known. The Duke had delightedly discovered the wealth of Italian instrumental music being turned out by Vivaldi and his confreres. In studying these works for performance by his Weimar forces, Bach converted several into brand-new pieces for keyboard alone—the ultimate compliment.

Prince Leopold von Anhalt-Cöthen, Bach's last noble patron, assembled a renowned orchestra prior to his inheritance of the title. Unfortunately, the woman he married in 1721 was no fan of music, and Leopold was forced to dismiss his ensemble, eventually causing Bach to seek the Cantorate in Leipzig.

At Weimar, Bach also encountered responsibilities more directly liturgical in nature. The musical heart of the Lutheran liturgy consisted of chorale melodies (most composed or

Germany as it is today, but in Bach's time, it was largely comprised of principalities and duchies and other what-have-yous the size of little Luxembourg to the left. Except for his student days in Lüneburg, Bach spent his life in the central German province of Thuringa, which was part of the Electoral Duchy of Saxony.

compiled by Luther and his immediate disciples), which served the Lutheran church as Gregorian chant served Roman Catholicism. To composers adept at draping basic tunes with garlands of new invention, these simple melodies provided at once an inexhaustible resource and the opportunity to work them into more elaborate compositions, be it as organ works (chorale preludes) or as the basis of extended vocal and choral compositions (cantatas).

Later in his career, as musical director at St. Thomas' Church in Leipzig, Bach devoted himself more prolifically to the enhancement of the body of Lutheran liturgy. Of the 300 cantatas he is known to have composed for church services—an awe-inspiring body of work comparable in grandeur to Michelangelo's Sistine Chapel—several of the most striking date from the Weimar years. By 1717, Bach had become one of Germany's most highly regarded organ virtuosos, both for his playing and his skill at improvisation. That same year, Prince Leopold of Anhalt-Cöthen, himself a critic and music-lover, approached the young man with an offer to work with the region's most renowned orchestra—the proverbial offer Bach could not refuse. Weimar's Duke struggled to forestall Bach's departure, going so far as to have him thrown into prison for nearly a month "for too stubbornly forcing the issue of his dismissal."

Finally sprung, Bach went to work at Cöthen's illustrious court. The court being Calvinist in religious orientation, Bach had no chapel duties; instead, his charge was to create and arrange music for

Leopold's superb group of musicians. In his five years at Cöthen, Bach produced the six brilliant *Brandenburg Concertos,* a number of concertos for violin, plus numerous sonatas, **suites,** and keyboard pieces, some meant for instruction (e.g., the *Well-Tempered Clavier* and *Anna Magdalena's Little Notebook,* composed for his second wife) but estimable for their artistic content as well.

But the Cöthen idyll likewise came to an end. Prince Leopold remarried, and his new bride lacked her predecessor's enthusiasm for music. Maria Barbara Bach also died, in 1720; a year later Sebastian married Anna Magdalena Wilcke, daughter of a court trumpeter at Weissenfels; with her he continued the production of talented composer-sons so handily begun with Maria Barbara.

In 1723, Bach accepted the prestigious post of Music Director of the City of Leipzig and Choirmaster of its Thomasschule; he would remain in Leipzig for 27 years, until his death in 1750.

CHAPTER 3

The Culmination: Bach at Leipzig

BACH FOUND THE ROAD to Leipzig to be roughly paved. Johann Kuhnau, previous holder of the posts of *"Director musices* at the two principal churches of St. Thomas and St. Nicholas and the same in the Pauliner-Kirche of the University, and no less Cantor at the Thomasschule," had died on 5 June 1722. The prolific and popular Georg Philipp Telemann had been hired away from Hamburg as Kuhnau's successor, but the offer of a fat pay increase persuaded him to stay put. "Since the best man could not be obtained," grumbled Appeals Councillor Platz in the minutes of the Leipzig town council's deliberations, "mediocre ones would have to be accepted." On 5 May 1723, the council found Johann Sebastian Bach "theologically sound" and he was duly elected. Less than one month later, the annals of the town council noted that the new Cantor and Music Director "produced his first music here, with great success."

Bach's statue as it stood out-side St. John's Church, Leipzig: Photographed in 1930, St. John's was damaged beyond repair by Allied bombing during WWII. The statue was subsequently moved.

No longer a noble's hired hand, Bach had become a political figure as well as a musician, a governmental appointee with some rank (if not all that much) in Leipzig's ruling hierarchy. That city, located at the confluence of three rivers about 120 miles south of Berlin, had its own noble history. Founded in the eleventh century as *Urbs Lipsicum,* it gained prestige as a mercantile center and the home of book publishing in the German-speaking lands. Its university, established in 1407, had garnered world-wide fame by Bach's time. Twice a year Leipzig staged an Imperial Trade Fair, where everyone of financial importance in Central Europe hobnobbed with everyone else.

The Leipzig post paid better than any of Bach's previous employment—not so much, however, as to prevent the composer from issuing a string of complaints. The correspondence throughout Bach's tenure sounded a sad and constant roundelay: Bach saddled with new chores without pay; Bach's orchestra reduced to seven players instead of the promised eighteen; Bach stiffed out of his usual fee for playing at weddings when a parishioner got married somewhere else; Bach nearly fired, deemed "incorrigible" by employers and colleagues alike for his incessant complaints.

For the most part, Bach's objections were justified. He and Anna Magdalena lived with their growing brood in a cramped space separated from the school dormitory by a thin wall. Six of the first eight children born to the Bachs in Leipzig perished from diseases brought on by the filth in their apartment. The rules of his employment forbade his leaving the city without permission.

The amazement, then, is not only the miraculous quality of the music Bach turned out in Leipzig but that he could compose at all. Compared to the output of his contemporaries—Vivaldi with his

Leipzig marketplace: A thriving mercantile town with its own university and choir school, Leipzig frequently used the marketplace for civic ceremonies. None was more spectacular, however, than the greeting made to King Augustus III in 1733: a grand salvo of 2200 muskets was fired by the town's militia in his honor.

almost 600 orchestral concertos, plus operas and religious music—Bach's totals are not quite staggering. What *is* staggering is the richness and variety in these works. Of the 300 or more cantatas he produced for Leipzig, some 200 survive; each is a kind of deep musical meditation, built around the chorale melody to be used in that day's church service, a discourse on both the melody and its text drawn out of Bach's own creative conscience. And while he indicated no interest in Italian opera (but then, he never lived in a town with an opera

Papa Bach

Prolific in more ways than one, Bach fathered 20 children: 10 died in childhood or infancy; one son (of six that survived) was feeble-minded but, according to his father, at least "inclined toward music;" another, Johann Gottfried Bernard, died at 24, at the start of a musical career; the others became renowned composers.

All four composer-sons received extensive music lessons courtesy of their father, as he had from his father, Johann Ambrosius. These lessons consisted of the most basic musical exercises: keyboard technique, above all, but also the study and analysis of music. Given the creative energy and potential for surprise in such works as the Inventions and the *Well-Tempered Clavier*, it is all the more exhilarating to realize that Bach created these first and foremost as teaching pieces for his children (especially his eldest, Wilhelm Friedemann): to explore the problems of performance, to master the myriad ways of counterpoint, and, particularly in the 24 pairs of preludes and fugues of the first volume of the *Well-Tempered Clavier*, to explore the nature and expressivity of all the tonalities in the house), the great *Passion* oratorios on texts from the Book of Matthew and the Book of John are intense dramas that need no staging to project their power. Of the forty-eight pairs of preludes and fugues that make up the two volumes of his famous *Well-Tempered Clavier*, each demonstrates some separate aspect of compositional and performance technique; again, no two works in the set are exactly alike. The tour de force of the so-called *Goldberg Variations* (composed by Bach for his student Johann Gottlieb Goldberg, who

harmonic system. Not until the twentieth century, in the case of Béla Bartók's *Mikrokosmos,* is there another example of a great composer at the height of his powers distilling the essence of his musical outlook into short pieces worthy of performance but designed for teaching.

The legend that Bach's four composer-sons turned their backs on the old man's music is somewhat unfair. True, all these men were part of new currents sweeping the cultural world midway in the eighteenth century. True, Carl Philipp Emanuel, acting out of contempt for fuddy-duddy musical ideals,

disposed of some of his father's printer's plates. True, the elegant, facile music of Johann Christian became so popular that people in his time generally took the name Bach to refer to him, not to his father. Yet both Philipp Emanuel and Johann Christian seem to have been visited later by pangs of conscience, and did what they could to perform their father's music in public. And the eldest, Wilhelm Friedemann, assimilated his father's music so much that, in the impoverished dementia of his later life, he could misrepresent his own compositions as Papa Bach's.

requested a musical cure for his employer's insomnia) is more than a set of glosses on a single theme; the work is an hour-long study in musical structure and mounting intensity, an exhaustive but exhilarating demonstration of the many kinds of music a single theme can generate. This remarkable panorama of his own musical style, the ability to bend the musical language of his time in so many startling ways, sets the legacy of Bach apart from the predictable craftsmanship of his prolific contemporaries.

Bach was not an innovator, in the sense of Claudio Monteverdi at the dawning of the Baroque or of Ludwig van Beethoven later on. His musical style had roots in the tradition of the German Baroque: he delighted in intricate counterpoint, in setting out musical problems the work in question would then resolve. His steadfast Lutheranism endowed his liturgical music with an

St. Thomas' Church and School, Leipzig: Bach's primary job title was Cantor of the Thomaskirche and the Thomasschule, where he was responsible for providing music, training the choir boys (all the students of the school), and teaching them Latin.

almost personal emotionality; it's impossible to experience the plangent sorrow of the arias in the *St. Matthew Passion* or the horrifying moment of Jesus' Crucifixion and Burial in the *Credo* section of the *B-minor Mass* without an awareness of the composer's hand close by.

Not all the good burghers of Leipzig recognized these qualities, of course. The influential critic Johann Adolph Scheibe, in his 1737 "Letter from an Able Musician," fumed against Bach's compositions, whose "bombastic and intricate procedures deprived them of naturalness and obscured their beauty by an excess of art." (It was later discovered, however, that Scheibe's rancor undoubtedly stemmed from his having lost out on an audition Bach had judged.)

Most of Bach's church music dates from his first years at Leipzig; the later choral works, even the overwhelming *Mass in B Minor*—composed to honor the Catholic king in nearby Dresden from whom Bach hoped to find employment—were generally recycled earlier German works. By 1729, Bach's clavier and organ music had seen the light of publication, and his fame began to spread throughout Europe. In that year, too, he took over the leadership of Leipzig's long-standing Collegium Musicum (sometimes called the Telemann Society), an amateur players' society Telemann had founded in 1702 when he worked in the city. Bach created a repertory of instrumental concertos for the collegium—some new and others consisting of movements from earlier instrumental and choral works—along with a number of cantatas on secular texts, most of them devoted to singing the praises of influential local dignitaries. These later earned him the honorary title of Court Composer to the Elector of Saxony.

Bach and Anna Magdalena enjoyed an untroubled domestic life in Leipzig; the youngest of their thirteen children, Johann Christian, grew into a major composer worthy of his half-brothers Wilhelm Friedemann and Philipp Emanuel. (Later in the eighteenth century, in fact, people took it for granted that the name "Bach" denoted Johann Christian rather than his illustrious father.)

In 1747, Bach traveled to Potsdam to see his son Philipp Emanuel (then employed as harpsichordist at the court of Frederick the Great) and brand-new grandson, and was greeted with high honors at the court. The King, himself no slouch as a flutist and composer, suggested a theme for an on-the-spot improvisation; Bach took the theme back to Leipzig, where he fashioned the tune into the lengthy

St. John's Church, Leipzig: A view of the church and its square.

Musical Offering, a compendium of several musical forms—some ancient, some in the style the King favored in his own music making.

Bach's final years in Leipzig were, in fact, given over to the kind of musical speculation the *Offering* typifies: a series of intensive explorations into the many permutations possible on a single musical idea. His last work bore the title *The Art of the Fugue* and was just that—a portfolio of differing treatments of an almost rudimentary D-minor phrase.

Bach's eyesight began to deteriorate during his last year. In March 1750, he was treated for cataracts by John Taylor, an itinerant British oculist whose operation likely hastened his death. Blind and ailing, the 65-year-old Bach continued work on the nineteenth fugue in *The Art of the Fugue* series, an elaborate contrapuntal exercise into which a Lutheran chorale melody and his own name (B A C H spells out four pitches in German musical notation) had been interwoven. He took final communion on 22 July, and passed away six days later. His widow, Anna Magdalena, died in poverty 10 years afterwards.

CHAPTER 4

The Infinite
Variety

o

OF ALL THE ARTS, music is the one most directly in command of time. Two singers in a Mozart opera may have entirely different things on their minds (check out the first duet in *The Marriage of Figaro*) yet can express their thoughts simultaneously because the music keeps them both together and apart. **Counterpoint** (or **polyphony**) is the technique whereby several lines of music go on at once and still maintain their individuality. Counterpoint had been devised almost a millennium before Bach's time; a ninth-century treatise describes "music composed of distinct but harmonious lines." Some of the earliest surviving polyphonies are truly amazing: a slow melody taken from a liturgical chant in one voice; a faster tune in another voice, often in a dancelike rhythm and with another text; and a third voice on top, frequently with a third text in French instead of Latin and in an entirely different rhythm!

By the Renaissance, counterpoint had become the lifeblood of sacred and secular music in the Western world. The idea of combining simultaneous lines of music in such a way that their coming together remained harmonious while preserving each line's individuality represented, to some composers, a challenge both scientific and aesthetic. The great works of Flemish masters in the late fifteenth and sixteenth centuries might present a situation in which a tune in one voice, played off against the same tune in a second voice, a different rhythm, and another direction (upside down or backward), and perhaps a third and a fourth voice proposing still further permutations—all preceded by the composer's cryptic hint at the proper "solution" to the work. Musicologists have yet to solve all the puzzle pieces from that period; whole college seminars have been devoted to unraveling the contrapuntal repertory of these composers.

Sixteenth-century Flemish composers such as Josquin Desprez and Roland Lassus (also known as Orlando di Lasso) worked in Italy as church choirmasters or music directors in noble's palaces, bringing their contrapuntal mastery to bear on the Italian repertory. An Italian madrigal, for instance, might have four voices simultaneously lament the pangs of amorous pursuit in four time frames. Their work drew the scorn of the Camerata intellectuals, and inspired a turn toward a more songlike, one-line-at-a-time kind of music than counterpoint.

The north, however, saw no such upheaval; counterpoint held sway. Composers in the early Baroque—Netherlands master Jan

The Heart of the Fugue

The word fugue suggests flight or, even better, pursuit, as in "fugitive." It turns up in Renaissance polyphony, referring to a theme's tendency to pursue itself—to appear in successive voices, in other words, at successive time intervals, and continue the process of never catching up with itself until the composer brings matters to a halt.

Baroque composers greatly elaborated and subtilized the nature of the fugue, heightening its obsessiveness, its ability to bear down on a single short theme and extract every glimmer of its expressive potential. It is safe to say, without exaggerating too much, that of Bach's hundreds of fugal compositions, no two are exactly alike. That's because Bach, more than any of his predecessors, had the genius to turn themes upside down, to expand or contract their duration, to play one theme off against itself in altered guise, and to periodically relax the terrific intellectual game playing, thus allowing the listener a moment's breath.

At times, however, the idea of fugue has gone out of fashion— the music of Bach's sons, for instance, emphasized simple melodies riding upon simpler accompaniments. But then Wolfgang Amadeus Mozart discovered Bach's music and started writing fugues and Ludwig van Beethoven turned the form into an overpowering dramatic outcry; in the twentieth century, Béla Bartók's music is drenched in the spirit of fugue. Not all composers accepted this ancient, complex musical form; Hector Berlioz, in his text for his *Damnation of Faust,* refers to it as "la bestialité en toute sa candeur!"—"bestiality in all its glory!"

Sweelinck and German Samuel Scheidt—turned the polyphonic style of the Renaissance choral music into instrumental works as well; out of their **fantasias, partitas,** and **variations** grew the music that shaped the thoughts of the young Bach, particularly the fugue. A complex but flexible musical form, the fugue consisted of the contrapuntal working out of a **subject** (or short theme) played in counterpoint with itself, with the learned manipulation relieved at times by simpler, less intricate **episodes.**

Those words represent the simplest description of a musical device that, in practice, lent itself to countless permutations. Instead of a single subject, a fugue might contain two or more, worked out in succession or simultaneously. The devices within the fugue seemed the logical descendants of the "puzzle pieces" of the previous century; a theme might return played upside down or backward, or at a different pace. The composer might precede the fugue with a freer section, possibly virtuosic in style, possibly improvisational. In the hands of the Baroque composers, this strictest of musical forms became the freest.

Accounts of Johann Sebastian Bach at age ten have him improvising fugues at the organ of his older brother and guardian Johann Christoph (thus, according to legend, incurring Christoph's jealousy). One miracle of Bach lies in his ability to assimilate the technique and spirit of the contrapuntal devices of the German Baroque, and in his making them work on a dramatic level that can thrill today's listener as it must have astounded those of his time.

Several streams of musical thinking converge in Bach's works, where they merge with his own visions. From his immediate forebears, especially organist and composer Dietrich Buxtehude, he learned the power of the mighty organ, the ability of a virtuoso performer to rattle the very gates of Heaven, the manner in which a grandiose contrapuntal exercise can roll through the expanse of a great church and into the very bloodstreams of its listeners. The organ compositions from Bach's early years as a professional composer at Arnstadt and Mühlhausen repre-

A Canon from The Art of the Fugue *(manuscript page): The collection Bach was working on when he died.*

sent the efforts of a flamboyant hell-raiser; his music crashes into expressive realms no composer had dared to explore. The first part of the *D-minor Toccata and Fugue* (famous for its gorgeous colorization in Disney's *Fantasia*) is a fine example; its fiery energy is an irresistible force, even without the help of the Disney artists. From his Italian contemporaries Bach learned the power of a haunting, unfolding line of melody, indelibly colored by the emotional richness of the underlying harmony, and colored further by the virtuosity of the singing voice or the solo instrumentalist. No previous composer had mastered the enormous emotional range that a line of melody could evoke: the whooping hilarity at the start of the *Magnificat;* the mystical, rolling dissonances in the first *Brandenburg Concerto;* the harrowing tragedy in Mary Magdalene's "Erbarme Dich" from the *St. Matthew Passion.*

Plunge in anywhere: take the opening chorus of the *St. Matthew Passion,* the Betrayal and Crucifixion of Jesus Christ as told by the Evangelist Matthew. The drama is immediately apparent in Bach's decision to divide his performing forces as a means of creating dramatic confrontation: two groups of instruments and two choruses, with the Narrator and Jesus as intermediate figures between the groups. The work opens with an orchestral invocation, the two ensembles joined in the exploration of a long, sorrowful line of melody, taken up by the full forces entering at intervals, group by group, with the same theme.

Then the first chorus enters with its orchestra, calling the "Daughters of Zion" to mourn over the body of Christ. Their melody maintains the mournful atmosphere, intensified as pairs of voices take up the melody in turn at a distance, as if to launch a full-fledged fugue: sopranos and altos first with one theme, tenors and basses with another. The drama intensifies as the second chorus and orchestra enter in conversation.

First: "See him!"
Second: "Whom?"
First: "The Bridegroom. Christ. See him!"
Second: "How?"

First: "The spotless Lamb."
Thus the listener is involved in two kinds of contrast: the counterpoint within the working out of the choral and orchestral parts as well as the exchanges between the first and second groups. These contrasts fill in both the real and the psychological space around the performers. As if that weren't enough, a third chorus of high voices (boys' or women's) floats above all this activity, with the slow chorale melody "O guiltless Lamb of God," an extraordinary dramatic touch

St. Matthew's Passion: *A manuscript page from the score.*

that seals the coiled-spring energy of the entire movement.

Another example of this confrontational, contrapuntal drama is the chorale movement from *Cantata No. 147,* known familiarly as *Jesu, Joy of Man's Desiring.* The layout here is simpler: the joy of Jesus' nearness is celebrated with a gently rolling tune in triplets, almost a pastoral dance, onto which is imposed the slower, steadier tune of the chorale. The energy stems not from the complexity of many elements crammed into one but from a sweetly flowing exaltation, a gentle alternation between the message of the chorale tune and the world's joyous reception of it.

Bach learned to make these elements work on a higher level of expressiveness than any composer before his time—*since* then as well. He is the one composer whose music never gives any sense of being old, new, or of any specific era at all. Perhaps this explains Bach's peculiar resilience to the Disney treatment, the Swingle Singers (who turned his keyboard pieces into scat choruses with jazz-combo backing), and to Peter Schickele's P.D.Q. Bach ("last and least of all the sons"). The infinite variety of Bach is only partially explained by where his music came from, or by where it has proven capable of going; the rest reflects his own genius.

CHAPTER 5

Eclipse and Rediscovery

o

DESPITE PREVAILING LEGEND, it is not quite true that Johann Sebastian Bach and his music fell into obscurity upon his death in 1750. His fame as an organist—a virtuoso and a master at improvisation—was firmly established throughout Europe. Connoisseurs still recognized the value of the elder Bach's mastery, despite a movement toward simpler, more accessible music. "At the very time when the world was beginning to degenerate in another direction," wrote the distinguished scholar F. W. Marburg in 1754, "when light melody-making was gaining the upper hand and people were becoming tired of difficult harmonies, the late Capellmeister was the one who knew how to keep the golden mean, and taught us how to combine an agreeable and flowing melody with the richest harmonies."

Even though Bach's major works were slow to achieve publication, major musical figures throughout the last decades of the eighteenth century made it a point to journey to Leipzig to inspect the composer's manuscripts and instruments. "The greatness that was my father's," wrote Philipp Emanuel in 1773, "was far too well known for a musician of reputation to let the opportunity slip of making the

Bach "Rediscovered"

Despite familiar legend, it is not exactly true that Bach's music lay gathering dust in the decades following his death. Anyone who cared to could easily put his hands on enough music to establish Bach's towering stature, for such key works as the *Well-Tempered Clavier* and many organ pieces saw publication in Bach's lifetime, while many more were rushed into print during the first decade after his death. Most serious musicians in Europe knew a fair amount about Bach in the last half of the eighteenth century. When Wolfgang Amadeus Mozart and Joseph Haydn came into the company of Vienna's leading Bach enthusiast, Baron Gottfried van Swieten, both showed in their music recognition of Bach's im-portance. Major public recognition, however, took longer.

In 1818, poet Johann Wolfgang von Goethe fell under the spell of Bach's organ music and consulted composer Carl Friedrich Zelter for help in understanding its complexities and intensity. Zelter was himself a Bach enthusiast; the contact with Goethe intensified his own love of the music. Zelter led performances of Bach's music in his home, which the young Felix Mendelssohn frequently attended. Sometime around 1827, Zelter showed Mendelssohn the real treasure in his collection, a hand copy of Bach's *Passion According to St. Matthew*. Zelter had jealously guarded the score, believing the outside world did not yet deserve so great a masterpiece. Something in the eighteen-year-old Mendelssohn apparently closer acquaintance of this great man."

Viennese noble, physician, and arts patron Baron Gottfried van Swieten, who reported in 1774 that Frederick the Great had told him about Bach and had performed parts of the *Musical Offering* the

convinced him that this young Messiah was the vehicle by which the work would reach the world.

An enthralled Mendelssohn set about planning the world's first hearing of this staggering master-work since Bach's time. That took place at the Berlin Singakademie on 11 March 1829 to a public acclaim that necessitated a repeat perfor-mance ten days later, thus launch-ing the public rediscovery of Bach.

What did that public actually hear, on those two winter evenings in 1829? Hardly a *St. Matthew Passion* that an "authenticity-ori-ented" modern audience would rec-ognize. There were cuts, along with reorchestrations and touch-ups in the sound; arias meant for one singer went to another. One critic wrote in ecstasy of the solo violin-ist's "big and rich tone."

However far Mendelssohn's perfor-mance may have strayed from Bach's own vision, his actions turned the history of worldwide musical consumerism onto a glow-ing new pathway. Philosopher Georg Wilhelm Friedrich Hegel, a listener at the performances, spoke of Bach's "grand, truly Protestant, robust and, so to speak, erudite genius, which we have only re-cently learned again to appreciate at its full value."

Thirteen years after his coup at the Singakademie and 90 years after the passing of its composer, Mendelssohn conducted the *St. Matthew Passion* at the St. Thomaskirche in Leipzig, the site of its original presentation. Bach's incomparable music drama had finally come home.

The reconstruction of Bach's head, based on his skeleton: Starting late in the 19th century, scientists began picking and poking at Bach's remains to determine why he was so brilliant. They measured his skull, the distance between his eyes, and the height of his forehead to reveal his physiognomy. The result of their investigation? Bach was brilliant.

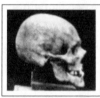

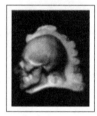

composer had sent him 25 years before, made the pilgrimage to Leipzig. A fervent music-lover, van Swieten assembled an impressive collection of manuscripts by both Bach and George Frideric Handel, and saw to it that his three protégés back in Vienna—Franz Joseph Haydn, Wolfgang Amadeus Mozart, and Ludwig van Beethoven—had access to these otherwise unknown works.

As early as 1782, soon after settling in Vienna, Mozart wrote to his father about discovering Bach's music at Baron van Swieten's home, and about taking manuscripts to his own home, where his wife "fell quite in love with the fugues" and begged her husband to write one for her. In 1789, Mozart visited Leipzig and heard some of Bach's choral music for the first time. "His whole soul seemed to be in his ears," an eyewitness reported. It takes little imagination to realize that these discoveries inspired the great interplay of counterpoint in Mozart's late works, most of all in the *Requiem.*

Further north in his native Bonn, the 13-year-old Beethoven astounded audiences with his playing of the *Well-Tempered Clavier,* a collection that also served him well in his early years as a keyboard virtuoso in Vienna. Throughout his life, in fact, Beethoven pushed the Bachian cause, arranging a benefit concert for Regine Susanna Bach (the last surviving daughter, then living in poverty) and lending his support (in vain) to a complete publication of the works. Hearing Bach's organ music while at Berka, a modest spa, the poet Johann Wolfgang von Goethe described the music as "the eternal harmony conversing within itself."

In Berlin on 11 March 1829, when the 20-year-old Felix Mendelssohn (already

Title page from the Well-Tempered Clavier, Book I: *Originally conceived as an exploration of the effects of refined tuning methods for the keyboard, the* Well-Tempered Clavier *was one of the young Beethoven's meal tickets as a piano virtuoso, first in Bonn and later in Vienna.*

esteemed as a composer and conductor throughout Germany) presented the first performances of the *St. Matthew Passion* since its composer's death, the cause saw its most significant advancement. But the work hadn't survived its first century unscathed, for Mendelssohn conducted an abbreviated, reorchestrated version of the music, a sort of midpoint between authentic Bach and the Romantic ideal. Still, Mendelssohn's brave act rekindled the Bach flame, and the composer's work suddenly found praise in perfor-

Bach in Performance

Soon after Felix Mendelssohn led the "rediscovery" of Bach's choral music, choruses the world over took up his music with the zeal of pioneers. Even before the Bach-Gesellschaft published the cantatas in something close to their "authentic" condition, some of the most attractive of them (including *Ein feste Burg*) were published and performances had flourished. In most cases, these performances would have sent today's scholars up the wall:

thickly rescored orchestration with horns and woodwinds added to make everything sound souped-up romantic, interpreters bent on emphasizing the beauty of it all with exaggeratedly slow tempos and even more blatant slowing down at the ends of movements.

The Romantics, in other words, seemed anxious to make Bach one of their own; contemporary scholarship, on the other hand, seeks to return Bach to something close to the aesthetic of his own time. The first recording of any of Bach's cantatas occurred in 1929, by a huge chorus in Barcelona mances, publications, and ecstatic critical essays by the likes of German composer Robert Schumann. In 1850, a century after Bach's death, a group of scholarly devotees, including Schumann, founded the Bach-Gesellschaft in Leipzig, dedicated to the gathering, editing, and publication of the complete works.

Not everybody expressed their delight, of course. French composer Hector Berlioz greeted a Bach performance as "ridiculous psalmody"; Friedrich Nietzsche pooh-poohed the welcoming of

singing in (!) Catalan, and turning the sound of *Christ lag im Todesbanden (Cantata No. 4)* into something resembling wet wool. The second complete recording of a cantata (*No. 106*, the *Actus Tragicus*) took place in Boston, ten years later, with a small chorus and orchestra with harpsichord; it was a huge stylistic forward leap.

Bach cantatas have since been recorded in copious quantity: mostly, as in these performances under Joshua Rifkin, with proper attention to the proportions that Bach might recognize. As Rifkin recognizes, however, this matter of "authenticity" goes only so far: Rifkin's instruments are fair copies of eighteenth-century models and his singers observe the interpretation of trills and other vocal gadgetry set forth in eighteenth-century treatises, but the audience is not in an ancient Gothic church and few ears are shocked by dissonance, as most have encountered Richard Wagner and the Beatles. Conductors seeking an "authentic" performance must adjust for inevitable discrepancies wrought by the passage of time; this chap Rifkin does that very well.

Bach into the nineteenth century. "He stands at the threshold of modern European music," fumed the German philosopher, "but he is always looking back toward the Middle Ages."

The contemporary view of Bach's music acknowledges that, pro or con, these early attempts to recognize the value of Bach were somewhat misguided. The Bach that Romantics took to heart was an impure product. Monster instruments that could roar like a full orchestra had supplanted the long-deteriorated organs of Bach's day. Arrangers ground out editions of the choral works with purring woodwinds filling in Bach's clean, spare orchestration; even when the "authentic" Bach became available through the editions of the Gesellschaft, some audiences preferred the woolly versions. Boston's Handel and Haydn Society, one of the first major American performing ensembles (founded in 1815 and still going strong), steered clear of the *St. Matthew Passion* for the first four decades of its existence, and then presented a version that merely told the story, omitting most of the arias. The idea of turning the organ works into riproaring exercises for Wagnerian-size orchestras was well under way when, in 1872, Boston critic John Sullivan Dwight exuberated over the "accent, individuality, distinctness, and color contrasts" of these gross distortions.

Right around the turn of the century, however, something happened to restore the music to its rightful respectability. Just when the Romantic musical language seemed ready to collapse beneath the weight of its own volume, French instrument maker Arnold Dolmetsch and Polish keyboard artist Wanda Landowska got an idea:

How to Tell Bach from the Others

The farther one gets from a historical time, the more the components of that time come to resemble each other. The eighteenth-century observers seemed to have had no difficulty, or so they imagined, in telling Bach's music apart from his great contemporary George Frideric Handel. English journalist Sir Charles Burney could write that his friend Handel was "the only great Fuguist exempt from pedantry . . ." while in Bach's music "even an easy and obvious passage [is] loaded with crude and difficult accompaniments."

Critics cannot speak so surely today. What is easier to spot, at least in contrapuntal music, is Handel's tendency to abandon his fugues and continue with a more harmony-oriented style once all the voices have been heard, as opposed to Bach's obsession with maintaining to the end the contrapuntal interweaving. Antonio Vivaldi's music has hardly any contrapuntal activity; listen instead for a melodic style built out of consecutive "building blocks": symmetrical sequences moving up and down the scale, often with great energy. Of the three almost exactly contemporary composers, Vivaldi is the most likely to charm the ear with the long-flowing melody thought of as "Italian." Try the slow movements of the four concertos that make up his *Four Seasons* for starters.

Truth be told, there is no hard-and-fast rule for distinguishing the top Baroque composers from one another, except for these few, very generalized sketches. Why bother? They're all great!

playing old music on instruments the composers might have actually heard. The "return" was only approximate; Landowska's harpsichords, made for her by the French piano factory Pleyel, were huge and clunky compared to Bach's own. But Landowska and her disciples had at least begun to increase the world's awareness of such things as the trills and turns that give Baroque keyboard music its vitality. A new generation of organ builders, inspired by none other than Dr. Albert Schweitzer, designed instruments that referred back to the low-volume cleanness of Baroque sonority. Slowly but ineffably, the authentic Bach made its return.

Today's Bach comes in many shapes and sizes, and manages to sound wonderful in all of them. Ponder for a moment the fate of one familiar work, the *D-minor Toccata and Fugue,* composed in Weimar for organ. (Or was it? Another school of thought on that piece has come up with a workable version for violin alone, claiming it as authentic.) Disney's *Fantasia* showcased the *Toccata* with lights and colors, in the irresistible pandemonium of Leopold Stokowski's orchestration. Does the work flourish best in that version, in the violin version, or as played on a clean-voiced reconstruction of a genuine Bach-period organ?

The question, of course, cannot be resolved. An "authentic" performance would require an "authentic" audience in an "authentic" environment, an audience that had never heard any music later than the time of this one toccata: no Mozart, no Wagner, no Beatles. Any performance, then, can only be an approximation.

The strength of Bach's music is just that, in fact. He has outlived the neglect of the late eighteenth century, the tamperings of the Victorians, the contemporary versions for rock combo, Moog Synthesizer, or the scats of the Swingle Singers.

More than any other composer of the past, Bach has served as source, inspiration, even role model to subsequent generations of composers. Throughout the nineteenth century, composers exhilarated by the Bach rediscovery consciously imitated his forms and methods: Mendelssohn, in a set of preludes and fugues for piano clearly influenced by the *Well-Tempered Clavier;* Johannes Brahms, in his last published work, a set of chorale preludes for organ. The two opposing twentieth-century innovators made a kind of peace with Bach: Igor Stravinsky in an expansion for chorus and orchestra on the *Canonic Variations,* and Arnold Schoenberg in his orchestration of the organ *Prelude and Fugue in E-flat* (the "St. Anne"). Both of Schoenberg's 12-tone disciples invoked the Bach spirit. Alban Berg introduced a Bach chorale harmonization in the closing measures of his *Violin Concerto;* Anton von Webern made his own setting of the final fugue from the *Musical Offering.* Brazilian composer Heitor Villa-Lobos created a series of *Bachianas Brasileiras* in which he blended the sound and spirit of Bach with Brazilian dance rhythms. In one remarkable outlook on Bach, composer-satirist Peter Schickele (also known as P.D.Q. Bach) has created an amalgam between the first prelude of the *Well-Tempered*

Clavier and the minimalist style of American composer Philip Glass; he calls the work *Einstein on the Fritz.*

No composer in history, in short, has been so jazzed up, watered down, electrified, and otherwise transmogrified, debated, and admired as this German provincial. But the ultimate wonder of Bach is his ability to appear to all generations as both romantic and scientific, melodic and objective.

CHAPTER 6

Music and
the Word

o

ON 31 OCTOBER 1517, German biblical scholar and religious reformer Martin Luther posted his famous declaration of church rebellion, in the form of ninety-five theses nailed to his church door at Wittenberg. Corrupted by the ease of making money, the Church at Rome had lost contact with the ranks of the faithful—or so Luther declared. He hoped to regain that contact by founding a new church, based on his own vernacular translation of the Bible. The Lutheran church conducted its services in the vernacular, lavishly enriched by an outpouring of music. Instead of Latin chants, which formed the traditional Roman liturgy, the Lutheran liturgy embraced a newly fashioned repertory of chorale melodies that similarly employed specific texts for each event in the church year. Luther, a musician of considerable talent, composed many of these chorale melodies himself; others he lifted from Latin chants as well as from popular melodies.

"Why should the Devil have all the best tunes?" Luther is said to have demanded.

Church song flourished as a splendid, expressive art in Europe's new Protestant churches. Every Sunday or feast day had its own chorale melody; each church's hired musician, whose job was to compose for the choir and improvise on the organ, had to weave the day's tune into a more extensive composition known as the *Haupt-Musik* (principal music). That piece, later known as the cantata, occupied a central position in the service.

The Passion

The central drama of Christianity— the Betrayal, Crucifixion, and Resurrection of Jesus—has also been the central media event for the faithful from the earliest times of worship. One of the earliest versions, traceable to at least the ninth century, took the form of dramatic dialogue between an Angel and the three Marys used in Easter services.

Angel: "Whom do ye seek in the sepulchre?"

Marys (in unison): "We seek Jesus of Nazareth, Who was crucified."
Angel: "He is not here. He is risen, as He said."

From these few words grew a tradition of drama to be performed both in the church and in theatrical spaces: reenactments of the drama, as well as meditations on its significance. A chant of lament to be sung by Mary Magdalene was a familiar feature; examples of this go back to the fifth century. By the seventeenth century, in both Catholic and Protestant cities, the commemoration of the Passion be-

The cantata immediately followed the Gospel reading in the service, and its text became a reflection on the substance of that reading—an elaborate, fanciful second proclamation of the Word. The music sought to amplify even further the symbols, secret meanings, and fanciful descriptive passages often found in the Gospel. (One charming example in Bach's *Herz und Mund:* John the Baptist "leaping and springing with joy" in his mother's womb to a spray of gleeful running notes as she prophesies the coming of Jesus to her unborn son.) The Lutheran cantata formed a musical and literary genre all its own.

came one of the two major theatrical events of the year (the other being the Nativity). In 1633, the Bavarian village of Oberammergau worked up its own reenactment of the Passion story, which included some incidental music. At that time, the villagers vowed to present their play at regular intervals to seek deliverance from a ravaging plague. They kept their vow, though the plague has long since ended.

The Passion's first musical settings grew entirely out of the story as told by the four Evangelists. Later, composers and poets added their own free inventions, greatly expanding the emotional range (not to mention the duration) of these reenactments. German composer Heinrich Schütz created his *Passion According to Saint Matthew,* which mingled the austere Lutheran chorale style and the emotional, contemplative manner of the Italian Baroque. Even though Schütz meant for his *Passion* to be sung without instrumental participation, its breadth of passion (in the more general sense) places it as the direct ancestor of Bach's two great Passion settings.

Typically, it consisted of biblical passages (or close paraphrases thereof) sung as **recitatives** interspersed with arias and choruses meditating on the significance of those passages; these often reached a high level of spiritual eloquence. By the time Bach undertook his first liturgical compositional responsibilities—at Weimar, sometime around 1714—his predecessors had created a large cantata repertory throughout the Lutheran realm, some works jealously guarded within a specific church, others in circulation.

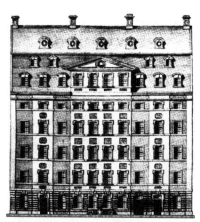

St. Thomas's School. The choir school was a descendant of the cathedral school of the Middle Ages. In exchange for room, board, and education, the boys were expected to sing at the city's four churches, at weddings, funerals, and various civic ceremonies.

Thus, the creation of sacred cantatas occupied the major part of Bach's churchly duties. The Weimar church expected him to produce at least one cantata every month, and he did so with great skill during the first two years as Concertmaster (1714-16); in 1717, a falling out with his employer caused a cessation of his church work. At Anhalt-Cöthen, where he worked from 1717-23, the Calvinist chapel made no compositional demands. At Leipzig, however, his production of cantatas resumed with immensely increased rapidity. In his first two years there, Bach wrote two weekly cantata cycles, well over 100 works altogether. After 1725, his production slackened, but by then he had amassed a musical backlog that would see him through several decades.

As a body of work, Bach's sacred cantatas (along with his settings of the *Passion* narration and the sublime *B-minor Mass*) form a study of one man's interaction with the nature of faith that has few parallels in the arts: Michelangelo's Sistine Chapel, Shakespeare's tragedies—what else? The solos in *Cantata No. 147*—the profound interplay between human words and the wordless

The B-minor Mass: *manuscript page. Composed for Augustus the Strong, Catholic King of Poland and Electoral Duke of Saxony,* the B-minor Mass *was one of the few examples of Bach's use of Latin in his religious music.*

solace of the single woodwinds—and the quiet ecstasy of the twice-intoned final chorale: it all adds to a dialogue on sorrow and comfort from deep inside a questioning soul. The exultant hurling forth of Luther's triumphant chorale turns *No. 80* into a "mighty fortress"; the melody, now ascendant, now bathed in the soft, mystical light of the final duet, becomes in itself a stupendous drama, a dialogue between opposites.

Bach, the story goes, had no great respect for the operas that earned fame and fortune for some of his contemporaries. Yet the interplay in these cantatas—between good and evil, hope and despair, man and his Maker—becomes an even higher level of theatrical confrontation, colored by the incredible resource in Bach's harmonies, musical drama expressive beyond the reach of any paintbrush.

Another thing to know about the Bach cantatas is that their numbering bears no relation to reality. In 1850, the 100th anniversary of Bach's death, the Bach-Gesellschaft (a large body of scholars,

Recycling in the Baroque

One of the quirkier issues surrounding Bach's catalog of works is the way in which some of his music—sometimes entire compositions—pops up in different places, frequently in different contexts. *Herz und Mund,* originally composed in Weimar for the last Sunday of Advent in 1717, is a case in point: Bach added four movements to texts by another poet and delivered the work as suitable for an entirely different church service. Similar things happen with the *Brandenburg Concertos,* sometimes decked out with new vocal music superimposed atop the orchestra, and the *B-minor Mass,* partly a collation of older cantata movements, with the liturgical Latin substituted for the German text.

At a time when music was scarcely being published and musicians like Bach had to come up with a halfhour's worth of performable material every week, musicians (as well as instrumentalists and singers) made do with whatever they had on hand. If Bach needed something—*anything*—for a postlude at the end of a Sunday service, he editors, and musicians) began collecting and publishing every known work by the Leipzig master. Until then, publication of Bach's works had been spotty: a huge array of instrumental and vocal music riddled with errors and romantic misinterpretation. The vast new scholarly venture sought to set matters straight.

In the matter of determining the chronology of the works, reality defeated the scholars. Bach, after all, was essentially one of thousands of eighteenth-century artisans working for employers who required a certain body of music to fill the needs of their private orchestras,

might conjure up entirely new music, or he might arrange a work by Vivaldi for the organ. When the Telemann Society presented a concert at Zimmermann's coffeehouse in Leipzig, he pulled out his fourth *Brandenburg* and refitted it for the present soloists. And when, toward the end of his life, Bach attempted to put his music into some kind of order, he took two portions of a Mass he had composed for King Augustus the Strong in the early 1730s, adapted a *Crucifixus* he had written 35 years before in Weimar, and ransacked other corners of his catalog to create the *B-minor Mass*.

Bach's employers expected him to compose, adapt, and transcribe (be it his music or someone else's)—whatever it took to "arrange" the music for the city and her churches, as is stated in his contract with Leipzig's town council. All in all, Bach's approach was a far cry from the quest for originality and novelty that describes much of the musical world today. But who noticed? Without recordings or videos or mass-produced song sheets, only a true aficionado could remember a piece heard just once five or ten years before.

soloists, and chapel choirs. The notion that this music could be, deserved to be, or needed to be preserved for posterity had not yet been formulated. Bach never thought to date his manuscripts or catalog his works, a practice that came into being decades after his passing.

Yet the Bach-Gesellschaft needed some way of listing the treasures over which they had assumed proprietorship. In the case of Bach's known sacred cantatas, the idea of assigning a chronological numbering system failed for at least two reasons: Bach's negligence in cataloging or dating his compositions and his practice of recycling cantata movements or even entire works. For example, *Cantatas Nos. 80* and *147* (both from Bach's time in Leipzig) contain recycled material from earlier cantatas composed during Bach's employment in Weimar.

The numbering of the cantatas, therefore, is totally arbitrary, a convenience that has nothing to do with history. *No. 147* in its final form dates from Bach's first years in Leipzig, while *No. 80* was composed about 10 years later. *Cantata No. 1* is a relatively late work, while *No. 4* is one of the earliest.

So forget the numbers and just listen to the music, for it carries the clearest message.

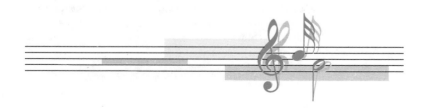

Play by Play:
Cantatas 147 and 80

As a composer for the Lutheran church, Bach mostly prepared cantatas for the liturgical year. The cantata (derived from the Italian "to sing") is first and foremost a vocal work, written generally for soloists with instruments and sometimes a chorus. It is, in Bach's hands, a multi-movement form comprised of choruses, recitatives, arias, and chorales. In their original settings, the cantatas represented joint efforts between the musicians, chorus, and congregation. Musicians performed the choruses, recitatives, and arias, while the congregation sometimes joined in on the chorales—an unlikely practice in *No. 147*, where the melody appears as a **cantus firmus** over a richly melodic and harmonic orchestral setting, but more than likely in the closing movement of *No. 80*, where Bach establishes the hymnlike motion in both the vocal and orchestral writing. In the recording featured here, Joshua Rifkin and the Bach Ensemble chose to perform both the choruses and chorales with only the vocal soloists.

Cantata No. 147: *Herz und Mund und Tat und Leben,* for the Visitation of the Blessed Virgin Mary (July 2)

Scoring: *Oboes I & II, oboe d'amore, oboe da caccia I & II, bassoon, trumpet, strings, and continuo; soprano, alto, tenor, and bass solo, four-part mixed chorus.*

The ancestry of this cantata is easy to trace. Its first form dates from Bach's Weimar years, when its text was published in a collection of the writings of Salomon Franck, Bach's principal literary collaborator at the time. The work was originally intended for the Fourth Sunday of Advent, the Sunday before Christmas; the gist of Franck's exhortatory, moralistic text concerns the duty of all people on earth to prove themselves worthy to greet the Saviour's arrival.

No one knows whether this first version of *Herz und Mund* ever saw the light of performance at Weimar. In any case, Bach took the manuscript with him to Leipzig, where it was finally performed, not during Advent but on 2 July 1723. The biblical text for that day (Luke I:39-56) also deals with arrivals: the pregnant Virgin Mary's visit to the elderly, unexpectedly expectant Elizabeth, mother of John the Baptist. Mary's arrival has a profound effect on Elizabeth as well as on her unborn son, who "bestirred, leaps and springs" within the womb at the happy tidings. An unknown poet added new texts to the Franck original, expanding the cantata to embrace this event.

It is, however, the setting of the chorale melody that endears this sublime, warmhearted music to its listeners. Atop a gently exultant, dancelike orchestral outpouring, the grand old chorale tune rides confidently, sending forth the loving message that Jesus abides eternally as the soul's joy. Long before the entire cantata made its way into the ever-expanding Bach repertory more than a century ago, this movement had earned its place as a piano arrangement (familiarly known as *Jesu, Joy of Man's Desiring*) by Dame Myra Hess (expected as the final encore at virtually every recital she gave).

Even Bach must have known he had a hit on his hands, for in the cantata's final form, this one movement occurs twice.

Track 1: **Chorus**

Herz und Mund und Tat und Leben	Heart and voice and deed and life
muß von Christo Zeugnis geben	must give witness to Christ
ohne Furcht und Heuchelei	without fear or hypocrisy,
daß er Gott und Heiland sei.	proclaiming Him God and Saviour.

In the fullness of Bachian sonority at its most resplendent [T1/i1, 0:00], trumpet and oboes summon the listener's attention with a fanfarelike theme, riding above the swirl of the strings. Those who know Bach's *Brandenburg Concertos,* especially the brassy splendor of the first two, will recognize the mood here.

Each section of the four-part chorus enters in turn in fugal succession [T1/i2, 0:33]: soprano, alto, tenor, and bass, each voice with the main theme, somewhat similar to the trumpet fanfare, spreading out in elaborate, breathless coloratura and coming eventually to a breathing point.

At [T1/i3, 1:34], orchestra and chorus reach a moment of punctuation but at [T1/i4, 1:41] quickly move on to a new kind of sound. Short melodic fragments bounce back between pairs of voices—soprano and alto answering tenor and bass.

Marvelous word painting! [T1/i5, 2:08] Bach's way of setting off high-emotion words by sudden darkening of the harmony is one of his miracles. Listen at this point to how the word *Furcht* (fear) evokes a deeper coloration than the rest of the text.

Without a real break [T1/i6, 2:43], the music moves on to a climactic final section. The bass starts it off with a rerun of the fugal theme heard at the start. The other voices join in (bass, tenor, alto, soprano—a reversal of T1/i2), and the musical activity overall is more intense.

[T1/i7, 3:39] returns to the brilliant orchestral introduction to round off this powerful opening movement.

The "Saviour's miracle," which Mary tells "all to herself," appears in Luke 1 as the text of the *Magnificat,* which Bach (and many other composers) also set as a separate composition.

Surrounded by a halo of string tone and the supporting continuo of keyboard and low strings [T2/i1, 0:00], the tenor sings a text that expands on the *Mund* (mouth) from the opening chorus. At

Track 2: *Chorus*

Gebenedeiter Mund!	O blessed voice!
Maria macht ihr Innerstes der Seelen	Mary lays bare her innermost soul with her thanks and praise;
durch Dank und Rühmen kund;	she tells, all to herself,
sie fänget bei sich an,	of the Saviour's miracle
des Heilands Wunder zu erzählen,	which he has wrought in her, his handmaiden.
was er an ihr als seiner Magd getan.	
O menschliches Geschlecht,	O humankind,
des Satans und der Sünden Knecht,	slave of Satan and of sin,
du bist befreit	thou art freed
durch Christi tröstendes Erscheinen	by Christ's consoling appearance
von dieser Last und Dienstbarkeit!	from this burden and servitude!
Jedoch dein Mund und dein verstockt Gemüte	yet thy voice and thy stubborn spirit
verschweigt, verleugnet solche Güte;	disavow and deny such mercy;
doch wisse, daß dich nach der Schrift	but remember that the scripture promises
ein allzu scharfes Urteil trifft!	an awesome judgment upon thee!

[T2/i2, 0:41], the harmony darkens, as the text depicts the "realm of Satan" from which the coming of Christ will deliver humanity.

At the very end [T2/i3, 1:29], Bach applies this striking dissonance to underline the "awesomeness" of the judgment awaiting those on earth.

By his use of obbligato solo instruments—in this case an **oboe**

Track 3: *Chorus*

Schäme dich, o Seele, nicht,	Be not ashamed, O soul,
deinen Heiland zu bekennen,	to acknowledge thy Saviour
soll er dich die seine nennen	should he call thee his own
vor des Vaters Angesicht!	before the eyes of the Father.
Doch wer ihn auf dieser Erden	But whoever on this earth
zu verleugnen sich nicht scheut,	does not hesitate to deny him
soll von ihm verleugnet werden,	shall by him be denied
wenn er kömmt zur Herrlichkeit.	when he comes to claim his glory.

d'amore—Bach often treats a vocal aria as a kind of duet, with one voice declaring the text and the other a wordless but profound reaction to those words. Here [T3/i1, 0:00], the reassuring, comforting text inspires music in the measure of a slow minuet, with the oboe taking the first "words," and the alto (here sung by a countertenor) joining the conversation [T3/i2, 0:30]. And a conversation it truly is, with constant alternation between instrumental and vocal passages.

The second stanza [T3/i3, 1:37], warning those who would deny the Redeemer, elicits a more passionate strain of harmony, with its dissonant chords underlying the idea of "denial." Notice also, near the end, the virtuosic setting of the word *Herrlichkeit* (glory).

As with the initial chorus [T3/i4, 3:00], the orchestral preamble is brought back to round off the form at the end.

Track 4:   *Recitative*

Verstockung kann Gewaltige verblenden,	Perversity can blind the mighty
bis sie den Höchsten Arm vom Stuhle stößt;	until the arm of the Lord casts them down;
doch dieser Arm erhebt,	yet this arm
obschon vor ihm der Erde Kreis erbebt,	though the world may quake before it,
hingegen die Elenden,	exalts the lowly
so er erlöst.	whom he redeems.
O hochbeglückte Christen,	O most favored Christians,
auf, machet euch bereit,	arise, make ready:
itzt ist die angenehme Zeit,	now is the time of gladness
itzt ist der Tag des Heils: Der Heiland heißt	now is the time of grace; the Saviour bids
euch Leib und Geist	you arm body and soul
mit Glaubensgaben rüsten,	with the gifts of faith.
auf, ruft zu ihm in brünstigem Verlangen,	Arise, call to him in fervent longing
um ihm im Glauben zu empfangen!	That ye may receive him in faith.

Again, the word painting throughout this recitative is a burst of slashing, contrasting colors. The Almighty hurls the proud ones from their throne; first the bass's vocal line [T4/i1, 0:00], then the buzzing of the continuo instruments draw the scene in vivid outline.

The action subsides [T4/i2, 0:44]; those of humbler mien are comforted as the long-awaited "time of grace" approaches. Then [T4/i3, 1:10] the music turns serene; the prophecy of Christ's coming resounds against clear skies.

Track 5: *Aria*	
Bereite dir, Jesu, noch itzo die Bahn,	Make ready, O Jesus, even now thy
mein Heiland, erwähle	path;
die glaubende Seele	My Saviour, elect
und siehe mit Augen der Gnade	the faithful soul
mich an!	and look on me with eyes of grace.

A rush of triplets [T5/i1, 0:00], played by the solo violin above an even-paced bass line, is obviously Bach's pictorialization of the pathway that brings the Saviour ever closer. Considering the importance of these triplets both here and in the next section, they might also signify the Holy Trinity.

Soprano and solo violin participate on an equal basis [T5/i2, 0:47]; as in Track 3, this is as much a duet as an aria.

The brief text repeats [T5/i3, 1:18] but to a different melodic strain, as if the singer had become impatient from awaiting the Saviour's arrival. The long notes on *bereite* have an insistent quality. A final time through this impatient text [T5/i4, 2:03], with the harmony much intensified.

Rounding off the aria, the opening orchestral passage [T5/i5, 2:57] returns verbatim.

Track 6: *Chorale*	
Wohl mir, daß ich Jesum habe,	Happy am I that I have Jesus;
o wie feste halt ich ihn,	O how firmly I shall hold him
daß er mir mein Herze labe,	that he may refresh my heart
wenn ich krank und traurig bin.	when I am ill and grieving.
Jesum hab ich, der mich liebet	I have Jesus, who loves me
und sich mir zu eigen gibet;	and entrusts himself to me;
ach, drum laß ich Jesum nicht,	ah, I'll thus not leave Jesus,
wenn mir gleich mein Herze bricht.	even if my heart should break.

Confident, content, serene; Bach implants his flowing chorale melody in a pastoral setting [T6/i1, 0:00] enhanced by the gentle, onward motion of the triplets and the brightness of trumpets, oboes, and violins among the solo instruments.

As the first verses of the chorale melody are sung [T6/i2, 0:15], the orchestra subsides, filling in between the vocal phrases as in a dialogue. In accordance with the traditional form of the chorale melody, the first part of the tune repeats [T6/i3, 0:42] but with different words.

Now the sung verses are joined by the triplets [T6/i4, 1:12], and the harmony darkens ever so slightly, to a minor key.

The opening strain returns [T6/i5, 1:36] but this time with the triplets continuing. As the orchestra continues [T6/i6, 1:51], the sustained low G (the key of the movement) strengthens the sense that the music has come full circle.

This ends the first part of the cantata. For its Leipzig performance, however, Bach added three movements, to texts by an author whose name hasn't survived, followed by a repeat of the chorale setting, the same music but with a different text.

This division of the cantata into two parts suggests the first part was performed after the reading of the Gospel, the second after the sermon.

Track 7: *Aria*	
Hilf, Jesu, hilf, daß ich auch dich bekenne	Help, Jesus, help me to acknowledge thee
in Wohl und Weh, in Freud und Leid,	in health and woe, in joy and grief,
daß ich dich meinen Heiland nenne	that I may call thee my Saviour
im Glauben und Gelassenheit,	in faith and confidence
daß stets mein Herz von deiner Liebe brenne.	that my heart may ever burn with thy love.

Again the triplets [T7/i1, 0:00], clearly seen by Bach as some kind of unifying force in the entire cantata. "Help," cries the singer, and the vocal line breaks up into short, urgent fragments. "In health and woe, in joy and grief" [T7/i2, 0:48]: listen to the vivid word painting. *Leid* (woe) comes out on a dissonance; at [T7/i3, 1:10] *Freud* (joy) is set as a flourish that is almost a giggle. Moments later [T7/i4, 1:20], the *Heiland* (Saviour) becomes a long, breathtaking coloratura line, while the several occurrences of *brenne* (burn with thy love) blaze ever more brightly.

Following a final quick cry for help [T7/i5, 2:19], the aria ends with the expected return of the instrumental prelude.

Track 8: ***Recitative***	
Der höchsten Allmacht Wunderhand	The Almighty's wondrous hand works in the hidden places of the earth.
würkt im Verborgenen der Erden.	
Johannes muß mit Geist erfüllet werden,	John must be filled with the spirit;
ihn zieht der Liebe Band	The bond of love tugs at him
bereits in seiner Mutter Leibe,	even in his mother's womb,
daß er den Heiland kennt,	so that he may know his Saviour
ob er ihn gleich noch nicht	even though he cannot yet
mit seinem Munde nennt.	call him by name.
Er wird bewegt, er hüpft und springet,	He stirs, he leaps and springs
indem Elisabeth das Wunderwerk ausspricht,	as Elizabeth proclaims this marvel,
indem Mariae Mund der Lippen Opfer bringet.	as Mary speaks the offering of her lips.
Wenn ihr, o Gläubige, des Fleisches Schwachheit merkt,	If ye, o faithful, mark the weakness of the flesh,
wenn euer Herz in Liebe brennet	if your heart burns with love
und doch der Mund den Heiland nicht bekennet,	and yet you do not acknowledge the Saviour,
Gott ist es, der euch kräftig stärkt,	it is God who shall give you great strength;

| er will in euch des Geistes Kraft erregen, | he shall awaken in you the power of the spirit, |
| ja, Dank und Preis auf eure Zunge legen. | lay thanks and praise upon your tongue. |

The recitatives in the Bach cantatas seldom serve merely to dispatch a lot of text quickly (as they often did in the Italian opera of the time); they embody some of the most complex and surprising of all his vocal writing. Here is a profound example [T8/i1, 0:00], two oboe da caccia (deeper toned and more resonant than both the customary oboe and the oboe d'amore used in *No. 3*) form a resonant, mellow commentary as the alto (countertenor) sings of Mary's visit to Elizabeth and of the unborn John the Baptist leaping in Elizabeth's womb (which the wind instruments unmistakably reenact) [T8/i2, 0:49].

With perfect logic (at least in eighteenth-century terms), this anecdote leads to yet another exhortation to acknowledge the source of worldly strength [T8/i3, 1:14].

Track 9: *Aria*

Ich will von Jesu Wundern singen	I will sing of Jesus' wonders
und ihm der Lippen Opfer bringen,	and bring him my lips' offering;
er wird nach seiner Liebe Bund	he will impose his love's command
das schwache Fleisch, den irdschen Mund	on my fainting flesh, my mortal voice
durch heilges Feuer kräftig zwingen.	with his holy fire.

As with the opening chorus in Track 1, the orchestral outburst that begins this final aria is hair-raising and complex: trumpet, oboes, and the full string section in a rousing, triumphant preamble [T9/i1, 0:00]. The aria [T9/i2, 0:28] is likewise spellbinding. Listen especially for the descriptive words *Opfer* [T9/i2, 0:38] and *Feuer,* and how Bach whips his bass soloist into something of a frenzy with long, breath-consuming coloratura passages. There is new, powerfully descriptive music for "fainting flesh" and "mortal voice" [T9/i3, 0:55] and a wonderful dissonance at [T9/i4,1:33] on "fire."

A final statement of the text is again full of *Kraft* (power) [T9/i5, 1:44] and *Feuer* (fire). Bach's brilliant orchestra, exulting again with the music that began this aria, now brings it to a close [T9/i6, 2:14].

Track 10: *Chorale*

Jesu bleibet meine Freude,	Jesus remains my joy,
meines Herzens Trost und Saft,	The comfort and libation of my heart;
Jesus wehret allem Leide,	Jesus wards off all sorrow
er ist meines Lebens Kraft,	and is the strength of my life,
meiner Augen Lust und Sonne,	the joy and sun of my eyes,
meiner Seele Schatz und Wonne;	the treasure and delight of my soul;
darum laß ich Jesum nicht	hence I'll not let Jesus
aus dem Herzen und Gesicht.	from my heart and sight.

Set to the same music as Track 6, final words of peace, faith, and confidence.

Cantata No. 80 *("Ein feste Burg ist unser Gott,")* for the Feast of the Reformation (October 31)

Scoring: *Oboe I, II, III, strings and continuo; soprano, alto, tenor and bass soloists, four-part chorus.* (N. B.: the trumpets and kettledrums heard in a few recordings were added by Wilhelm Friedemann Bach some years after his father's death.)

Of the hundreds of chorale melodies compiled or composed by Martin Luther and his colleagues, *Ein feste Burg* ("A Mighty Fortress") came to reign above all others as the pristine symbol of the Reformation. Long after Bach's time, the tune held that stature; it appears in the peroration of Felix Mendelssohn's "Reformation" *Symphony (No. 5)*; it is the defiant chant thundered forth by the rebellious Protestants in Giacomo Meyerbeer's opera *Les Huguenots*.

As with *No. 147*, the first version of this cantata lies buried in the small body of works Bach created during his service at Weimar, this one composed specifically for the Lenten cycle in 1715, bearing the title *Alles, was von Gott geboren* ("Everything born of God") and listed as *No. 80a* in the complete catalog. In that work, Luther's chorale melody showed up in two of the movements, thus serving a lesser role than in this grandiose final version. Piecing together the flimsy evidence that survives from all phases of Bach's creative life, scholars have surmised that Bach probably composed the final version of the work for the Feast of the Reformation (31 October) in 1734.

Luther's striding, triumphant melody, its first nine notes virtually a fanfarelike proclamation in themselves, becomes an unmistakable presence wherever and whenever it resounds. (Is it also the opening motto of Robert Schumann's "Spring" *Symphony?* The first theme of Franz Peter Schubert's recently discovered *Tenth Symphony?* The matter is, at least, arguable.) In this stupendously designed cantata, the melody appears in four of the eight movements: two (*Nos. 1* and *5*) as gigantic, wonderfully elaborate contrapuntal settings surrounded by the exultant blaze of the orchestra; one (*No. 2*) as a dialogue between the soprano's singing of the tune itself and the bass singer answering with a freely contrived variant of both tune and text; and one (*No. 8*) in the simplest, hymnlike four-part harmonization, as a sort of resolution to the earlier musical conversations.

Considering that the chorale melody for each day's church service served as the generating force for the cantata, it is fascinating to observe the variety of ways Bach devised for treating that given melody, just as Bach's poet-collaborators could produce elaborate verbal tropes that subjected the bare Lutheran texts to remarkable extensions.

Ein feste Burg belongs to what are known as "chorale cantatas," works in which the melody becomes the prominent constructive force in all or most of the entire work. The so-called *Easter Cantata* (*Christ lag im Todesbanden, No. 4*) is probably the best known of the sacred cantatas; there the solemn chorale tune becomes the basis for all seven movements. In *No. 147* (*Herz und Mund*), the chorale melody occurs only in the sixth movement, repeated verbatim in the tenth; the rest of the work is a meditation on the text of the chorale—not on its actual tune.

Track 11: ***Chorus***

Ein feste Burg ist unser Gott,	A mighty fortress is our God,
ein gute Wehr und Waffen;	a trusty shield and sword;
er hilft uns frei aus aller Not,	he sets us free from every need
die uns itzt hat betroffen.	that ever did beset us.
Der alte böse Feind,	The ancient evil fiend,
mit Ernst er's itzt meint,	doth compass us around,
groß Macht und viel List	with might and craft
sein grausam Rüstung ist,	in grimmest armour clad,
auf Erd ist nicht seinsgleichen.	on earth he has no equal.

A mighty shout proclaims the resonance of Lutheran faith [T11/i1, 0:00] but without the orchestral preparation found in Track 1. The four voices of the chorus enter one by one (as in a fugue), each voice doubled by an orchestral instrument of approximately the same register, while the cello rumbles along in a continuous accompanying melody also clearly derived from the chorale tune. First, the tenor, with viola; then alto [T11/i2, 0:09], doubled by the second violin; then soprano [T11/i3, 0:18], doubled by the first violin; and finally the bass [T11/i4, 0:27], with the cello now content to abandon its independent ways and join the bass's vocal line.

By now [T11/i5, 0:36], a four-part contrapuntal treatment involving both chorus and orchestra is in full swing, with the soprano's elaborate coloratura and the oboes piercing the busy vocal texture with an emphatic statement of the chorale theme.

Bass and soprano continue the imitative treatment of the theme [T11/i6, 0:51], but the other voices and instruments are, for the moment, off on their own. The two oboes add their penetrating voices to the texture once again, as this section seems to wind down [T11/i7, 1:18].

Following traditional practice, the third and fourth lines of Luther's text (starting *Er hilft uns frei*) are set to the same music as the first two [T11/i8, 1:37].

A new strain to a new text [T11/i9, 3:13]. As before, the four voices enter in fugal style: bass first, followed upward by tenor, alto, and soprano. Notice the interesting rhythmic setting of the first words (*Der alte böse Feind*), with the *alte* stretched out and the *böse* in **syncopation** against the regular pulse. Compare that with the final chorale (Track 18), in which the word and music rhythms are more "regular"—no doubt to facilitate the congregation's complete participation in the singing.

Word painting! On this final repetition of *Der alte böse Feind* [T11/i10, 3:48], the harmony turns sour, showing "the ancient evil fiend" in his true colors.

One has to admire Bach's sublime sense of balance, in matters large and small. The first phrase of this new strain [T11/i9, 3:13] is rhythmically active, and so it is counterbalanced by this slower answering phrase [T11/i11, 3:53].

The sense of activity is intensified [T11/i12, 4:24]. How? Mostly by shortening the elements in the dense contrapuntal texture so that consecutive voices answer each other at a shorter time interval.

Again, as contrast, Bach gives the next phrase (*sein grausam Rüstung ist*) a more spacious setting [T11/i13, 4:52]—longer notes spread further apart. Notice how, throughout this dazzling display of counterpoint, Bach maintains and emphasizes the two-repeated-note start of Luther's chorale theme.

Even here [T11/i14, 5:23], in this wonderfully rich setting of the final line of text (*auf Erd ist nicht seinsgleichen*), with the chorale melody broadened into a more flowing statement, the repeated-note melodic gambit is kept—with, however, the second of the two notes shortened.

The two oboes play in unison throughout this movement; only at the end [T11/i15, 5:51] are they set free to weave their own contrapuntal lines around one another. Listen, too, for a marvelous (and common) Bach trick: how the harmony seems to come unstuck at the final peroration. The music wanders momentarily into regions that don't relate to the key of D major you've been floating in for the past six minutes. But listen carefully; the lower instruments sustain a low D like a safety net under a trapeze artist. And right at the end, everything lands in that net, and just in time!

Track 12: ***Aria with chorale***

Alles, was von Gott geboren,	Everything born of God
ist zum Siegen auserkoren.	is destined for victory.
Mit unsrer Macht ist nichts getan,	Our power counts for nothing,
wir sind gar bald verloren.	we shall soon be lost.
Es streit' vor uns der rechte Mann,	The right man fights for us
den Gott selbst had erkoren.	chosen by God himself.
Wer bei Christi Blutpanier	Who to Christ's bloodstained banner
in der Taufe Treu geschworen,	has in baptism sworn allegiance
siegt in Christo für und für.	will gain victory in Christ forever.
Fragst du, wer er ist?	Dost thou ask who he is?
Er heißt Jesus Christ,	His name is Jesus Christ,
der Herre Zebaoth,	The Lord of Hosts;
und ist kein andrer Gott,	and there is no other God:
das Feld muß er behalten.	and He must hold the field.
Alles was von Gott geboren,	Everything born of God
ist zum Siegen auserkoren.	is destined for victory.

Bach called this marvelously contrived movement an "aria"; actually, it is a duet between a free-flowing aria for solo bass, expanding and celebrating the exultant Lutheran text, and the soprano (supported by the oboe) restating Luther's melody in a somewhat florid, rhythmically changed version. Before any of this, however, the strings and oboe provide their own exultation, a brilliant, trumpet-like introduction [T12/i1, 0:00]. Interesting point: even though Bach's son Wilhelm Friedemann devised a reorchestration of this cantata, adding trumpet and drums to reinforce the big choral movements, he left this one alone, apparently realizing that the mere suggestion of those instruments in this movement needed no further help.

The "conversation" is between the virtuosic, free-flowing bass melody [T12/i2, 0:25]—in which, for example, the soloist doesn't get to draw a breath for hours at a time (or so it must seem to him)—and the soprano's chorale melody, also luxuriant but broken into shorter phrases. The strings continue their trumpetlike accompaniment, while a solo oboe doubles the soprano for the most part, while adding a few virtuoso flourishes of its own. The impression is of a busy, crowded conversation on both the music and the text of Luther's resplendent chorale.

As in the first movement, the next two lines of the chorale text [T12/i3, 1:11] are set to the same music as the first two.

As the soprano moves along through the chorale (*Fragst du, wer er ist?*) [T12/i4, 1:54], the oboe becomes increasingly independent, relating to the vocal line but with new virtuosic flourishes.

As if to further emphasize the message of the text (the promise of victory to those baptized in Christ), the bass takes on these rather operatic leaps in his vocal line [T12/i5, 2:40], while the soprano colors her final exhortation with a striking dissonance [T12/i6, 3:18].

The orchestra returns with its original music to round off this movement [T12/i7, 3:34].

Track 13: *Recitative*

Erwäge doch,	Consider well,
Kind Gottes, die so große Liebe,	O child of God, this love so great:
da Jesus sich	for Jesus has
mit seinem Blute dir verschriebe,	committed himself to thee with his own blood,
wormit er dich	and thus enlisted thee
zum Kriege wider Satans Heer und wider Welt und Sünde	in the war against Satan's host and against the world and sin.
geworben hat!	
Gib nicht in deiner Seele	Keep your soul free
dem Satan und den Lastern statt!	of Satan and depravity;
Laß nicht dein Herz,	let not thy heart,
den Himmel Gottes auf der Erden,	God's heaven on earth,
zur Wüste werden!	become a wasteland.
Bereue deine Schuld mit Schmerz,	Repent thy guilt in sorrow,
daß Christi Geist mit dir sich fest verbinde!	so that Christ's spirit join firmly with thee.

As is usual with texts dealing with sin and guilt and the Devil, the harmony [T13/i1, 0:00] is restless, dissonant, and disturbed; the vocal line, similarly, provides a jagged outline, with wide, expressive skips. Notice the harmonic unrest [T13/i2, 0:34] as the text takes up the matter of Satan and sin.

The music changes to a more even-flowing style [T13/i3, 1:04] in both the voice and the accompaniment as those on earth are exhorted to renounce all the aforementioned evil and join with Christ's spirit.

Track 14: **Aria**

Komm in mein Herzenshaus,	Come in my heart's abode,
Herr Jesu, mein Verlangen!	Lord Jesus, my desire!
Treib Welt und Satan aus	Drive out the world and Satan,
und laß dein Bild in mir erneuert prangen!	and let thy image shine renewed in me.
Weg, schnöder Sündengraus!	Be gone, vile sinful horror!
Komm in mein Herzenshaus	Come in my heart's abode,
Herr Jesu, mein Verlangen!	Lord Jesus, my desire!

After a brief instrumental anticipation [T14/i1, 0:00], the aria continues on the comforting, conciliatory mood struck at the end of the preceding recitative. The operative word here, as in many of Bach's sacred works, is *Verlangen* (desired one); it extends the notion of prayer, of hope, of reaching for something not yet attained but clearly coming, that stands at the core of the Christian faith. Here, that one word is greatly extended in the vocal line.

At [T14/i2, 1:51], the mood becomes more agitated; God's house is not yet cleansed of "sinful horror." "*Weg weg, weg weg,*" the soprano sings in sharp, bristling rhythm; the easiest translation is "scram!"

The opening vocal melody returns to round off the aria

[T14/i3, 2:22], followed by the same instrumental strain that had preceded it: ABCBA, in other words.

Track 15: *Chorale*

Und wenn die Welt voll Teufel wär	And if the world were filled with
und wollten uns verschlingen,	devils
so fürchten wir uns nicht so sehr,	desirous of devouring us,
es soll uns doch gelingen.	we would not be sore afraid,
Der Fürst dieser Welt,	for we must yet triumph.
wie saur er sich stellt,	The prince of this world,
tut er uns doch nicht,	however harsh he may seem,
das macht, er ist gericht',	can do nothing to us:
ein Wörtlein kann ihn fällen.	already he is condemned;
	one little word can fell him.

Bach added this tremendous choral movement, the centerpiece of the cantata, relatively late in the confusing history of the work. It forms a striking contrast with the three other parts of the cantata based on Luther's chorale. The first movement treats the first stanza of the chorale as a series of fugal entries for chorus; the second movement allots the tune to a soprano solo against a free vocal line for the bass; and the final movement, as is usual in a Bach cantata, consists of a straightforward, hymnlike setting. In this movement, however, the third stanza is sung by the chorus in unison, in a new rhythmic variant, surrounded by a rich and complex orchestral texture

[T15/i1, 0:00]. Compare this to the familiar setting of the chorale in *Herz und Mund* (Tracks 6 and 10), or to the famous "Wachet auf!" in *Cantata No. 140* that bears that name; in all three cases it's as if the central article of faith had been endowed with a glorious and sonorous halo.

Three oboe d'amore join the orchestra. (Wilhelm Friedemann Bach also added trumpets and drums here, as in the first movement, in his published edition, and translated the text into Latin—which would surely have sent Luther to an early grave.) For the only time in the cantata, the basic meter changes to a flowing 6/8 time: the time signature of pastoral movements, of boatmen's songs, and, often in Bach, to suggestions of joyous, churchlike ceremonies with the swinging of incense vessels. (Compare the opening chorus of the *Christmas Oratorio* or the *Sanctus* of the *B-minor Mass*.) Try swinging your arms to this music; it seems only natural—though probably not seemly in an early Reformist church.

The chorus takes up the first lines of Luther's hymn [T15/i2, 0:22], its line-by-line proclamation interrupted by grandiose orchestral outpourings. As before, the first phrase of the chorale repeats [T15/i3, 1:11] prior to the return of the second strain of the chorale tune [T15/i4, 1:56].

The short poetic lines, dealing once again with Satan's attempts to defeat the souls of the godly, are sprinkled with quick but startling harmonic twists—at [T15/i5, 2:11], for example, and again at [T15/i6, 2:26].

The final lines of the chorale once again assert the victory on earth [T15/i7, 3:01], and the orchestra returns [T15/i8, 3:11] with the swirling, breathtaking music that began this remarkable movement.

Track 16: *Recitative*

So stehe denn	So stand firm,
bei Christi blutgefärbten Fahne,	by Jesus' bloodstained banner,
o Seele, fest	O soul, stand fast
und glaube, daß dein Haupt dich nicht verläßt,	and believe thy captain will not desert thee,
ja, daß sein Sieg	yay, that his victory
auch dir den Weg zu deiner Krone bahne!	shall lead they also to a glorious crown!
Tritt freudig an den Krieg!	Step joyful into war!
Wirst du nur Gottes Wort	Wilt thou the word of God
so hören als bewahren,	not only hear, but keep,
so wird der Feind gezwungen auszufahren,	then shall the enemy retreat in shame;
dein Heiland bleibt dein Hort!	thy Saviour will remain thy shield!

Like the previous recitative (Track 13), this exhortation falls into two parts: Luther's call to arms [T16/i1, 0:00], with its virtuosic demands on the tenor and its sprinkling of dissonant harmonies to underline every point—notice especially the little virtuosic flourish [T16/i2, 0:27] on *freudig* (joyful)—followed by a gentler, more melodic passage [T16/i3, 0:46], comforting the happy warrior on the occasion of his victory, wrapped in the Word of God.

Track 17: *Duet*

Wie selig sind doch die, die Gott im Munde tragen,	How blessed are they who speak God's name;
doch selger ist das Herz, das ihn im Glauben trägt!	but more blessed still is the faithful heart.
Es bleibet unbesiegt und kann die Feinde schlagen	Remaining whole to trounce the foes,
und wird zuletzt gekrönt, wenn es den Tod erlegt.	It shall defeat death and thus be crowned.

Sheer beauty, the blend of alto and tenor, and of oboe da caccia and strings, joined in gentle **imitation** [T17/i1, 0:00]. The musical motion is very subtle here. Try to feel the way it shifts from three beats to the bar (the actual time signature) to the same 6/8 motion felt in Track 15's big choral movement.

The battle won, it is time to draw inspiration from such words as "blessed" and "faithful" [T17/i2, 0:36]. This is joyous music, quietly so, as the singers join in harmony while solo oboe and violin spin a kind of filigree around them.

The music is full of echoes: the singers echoed by instruments [T17/i3, 1:20] and, one phrase later, tenor and alto imitating each other.

A second melodic strain [T17/i4, 1:58]: notice the naive but charming word painting—the long note at [T17/i5, 2:11] on the word *bleibet* (remains) and the way the oboe echoes that held note a few bars later [T17/i6, 2:30].

A serious moment, as *Tod* (death)—in a period of harmonic unrest—lies vanquished [T17/i7, 2:56] before the oboe and strings return to round off this utterly lovely movement [T17/i8, 3:03].

Track 18: *Chorale*

Das Wort sie sollen lassen stahn	Let them ignore the word:
und kein Dank dazu haben.	No thanks will come to them.
Er ist bei uns wohl auf dem Plan	He is beside us in the troop
mit seinem Geist und Gaben.	with his spirit and his gifts.
Nehmen sie uns den Leib,	Let them take our body,
Gut, Ehr, Kind und Weib,	wealth, honor, child and wife
laß fahren dahin.	let all be lost;
Sie habens kein Gewinn;	still they cannot win:
das Reich muß uns doch bleiben.	his kingdom shall remain ours.

The final stanza of Luther's hymn is delivered "straight," in Bach's original scoring: four-part chorus and strings [T18/i1, 0:00]. (Some recorded versions enlist the three oboes here as well, but this performance honors Bach's first inclinations.) The form is traditional; it follows the rubrics for German song that go back to the Middle Ages (and which are amusingly argued by the elder pedants in Wagner's *Die Meistersinger*): an initial strain (A) which is then repeated; a second strain that relates somewhat to the first (AAB overall, but with the second half of "A" and the second half of "B" thematically related). Complicated? Well, Wagner didn't think much of it, either.

Basic Bach:
The Essential Recordings

o

N.B.: The "BWV" ("Bach Werke Verzeichnis") identifications in parentheses after each work refer to the numbering in the Bach-Gesellschaft publication of the complete works. They have nothing to do with chronology, merely their order of publication.

1 **Cantatas 80** *(Ein feste Burg ist unser Gott)* and **147** *(Herz und Mund und Tat und Leben)*. Joshua Rifkin conducting the Bach Ensemble, with Jane Bryden, soprano; Drew Minter, countertenor; Jeffrey Thomas, tenor; and Jan Opalach, bass. L'Oiseau-Lyre 417 250-2.

See the Play by Play chapter for a detailed journey through these works.

2 *Organ Works: Toccata in D Minor,* (BWV 565); *Passacaglia in C Minor,* (BWV 582); *Preludes and Fugues in D,* (BWV 532); *in A Minor,* (BWV 543); *in E-flat,* (BWV 552). Organist Daniel Chorezempa at Our Lady's Church, Breda, for the first four works, and at the Bovenkerk, Kampen, The Netherlands, for the last. Philips 422 965-2.

Bach's musical visions had been formed in the organ loft, from a succession of teachers and idols. Dietrich Buxtehude represented one of the latter, and the story is often told of the 20-year-old Bach going AWOL from his Arnstadt post to make a pilgrimage (barefoot in the dead of winter, fancier legends have it) to hear the towering organ virtuoso ensconced at his mighty instrument in Lübeck.

The far-flung fantasies of Bach's greatest organ works, most dating from his early years at Arnstadt and Weimar, clearly show the influence of Buxtehude's extroverted flamboyance: nowhere more thrillingly than in the *D-minor Toccata and Fugue* (thrice-famous from its use in Disney's *Fantasia*). But the working out of such pieces as the stunning *C-minor Passacaglia and Fugue* likewise shows the contrapuntal mastery that became Bach's unique possession.

One work in this collection is of a later date: the majestic *Prelude and Fugue in E-flat* (the "St. Anne"), which appeared in Volume 3 of the *Klavierübung (Keyboard Practice)* that Bach compiled and published in Leipzig. The two parts of the work provide the frame for a marvelous collection of chorale preludes, contrapuntal treatments by Bach of Lutheran chorale melodies called, as a whole, *The Lutheran Organ Mass.* By themselves, the Prelude and Fugue form one of the peaks of Bach's genius, music so powerful that, as Bach had paid tribute to Vivaldi by orchestrating his music, no less a figure than Arnold Schoenberg orchestrated this stupendous work.

Track 1:	
Toccata and Fugue in D minor	
0:00	Toccata: introduction
0:43	Thematic group A
1:12	Thematic group B
2:01	Thematic group A (modified)
2:47	Fugue: first entrance (beginning of exposition)
2:52	Second entrance
3:12	Third entrance
3:46	Fourth entrance
4:13	Non-fugal interlude
4:37	Partial entrance
5:21	Partial exposition of fugue
5:46	Episode
6:15	Partial exposition
6:44	Episode
6:57	Partial entrance
7:25	Non-fugal coda

Track 2:	
Passacaglia and Fugue in C minor	
Set of variations over repeating bass line	
0:00	Passacaglia: exposition in bass line
0:23	First variation
0:45	Development
1:06	Second variation
1:28	Third variation
1:48	Development
2:10	Fourth variation
2:29	Development
2:49	Further development
3:28	Fifth variation
3:47	Development
4:04	Further development
4:23	Sixth variation (similar to fourth variation)
4:42	Development
5:02	Seventh variation

5:23 Eighth variation

5:44 Ninth variation

6:03 Tenth variation

6:25 Eleventh variation

6:44 Development

7:11 Fugue: first entrance

7:26 Second entrance

7:44 Third entrance

7:57 Fourth entrance

8:13 First variation

9:27 Second variation

10:00 Third variation

10:31 Fourth variation

10:56 Fifth variation

11:37 Sixth variation

12:11 Coda

Track 3:
Prelude and Fugue in D

0:00 Prelude

0:30 Thematic group A

1:02 Thematic group B

1:40 Variation

3:24 Thematic group C

4:50 Fugue: first entrance

5:04 Second entrance

5:22 Third entrance

5:38 Fourth entrance

6:41 Stretto

7:59 Series of "false" entrances

8:30 Stretto

9:43 Final entrance

Track 4:
Prelude and Fugue in A minor

0:00 Prelude: thematic group A

0:15 Thematic group B

0:23 A and B alternate

1:36 Thematic group A (return)

2:22 Variation

3:04 Fragments of group A (return)

3:47 Fugue: first entrance

4:00 Second entrance

4:23 Third entrance

4:54 Fourth entrance

5:42 "False" stretto

6:00 Episode

6:32 Non-fugal interlude

8:01 "False" stretto (based on first entrance)

9:36 "False" stretto (based on second entrance)

9:59 Coda

3 ***Brandenburg Concertos No. 1 in F,*** (BWV 1046); ***No. 2 in F,*** (BWV 1047); ***No. 6 in B-flat,*** (BWV 1051). Sir Neville Marriner conducting the Academy of St. Martin-in-the-Fields, with Alan Loveday and Iona Brown, violins; David Munrow, recorder; Neil Black, oboe; and Barry Tuckwell, horn. Philips 426 088-2.

As so often happens with Bach, works he may have written to explore a certain musical problem turn out to be remarkable listening as well. During his time as court musician at Cöthen, Bach composed a set of orchestral works, each for a different combination of instruments, and thus each a study in orchestration and sonority. He dedicated the set to a nearby potentate, the Marquis of Brandenburg (though no one knows if any of this superb music ever reached the Marquis' ears—or any other ears of the time).

Two of the three works here in the first of two discs exploring the whole set are wonderful studies in brass scoring at its most exuberant and in the possible relations between horns, winds, and strings. Both *No. 1* and *No. 2* take the brass instruments up into the stratosphere of their range—listen especially for the (literally) breathtaking work in *No. 2*. *No. 6* is just the opposite, a study in the amazing range of sonority that can come from an ensemble of nothing but low strings. After you've heard this work, dig out a couple of colorful modern rip-offs: the first and fifth *Bachianas Brasileiras* by Brazil's Heitor Villa-Lobos, for an ensemble of eight cellos (with, in *No. 5*, the addition of a soprano).

Tracks 1-5:

Brandenburg No. 1 in F

Track 1:
Allegro

0:00 Thematic group A

0:35 Thematic group B

1:15 Thematic group A: partial
    return, D minor

1:39 Thematic group C

1:58 Thematic group A: partial return

2:13 Thematic group B: partial return

3:21 Thematic group A: complete
    return

Track 2:
Adagio

0:00 Theme: oboe solo

0:26 Theme: violin solo

0:52 Interlude: theme in bass
    instruments

1:07 Variation

1:56 Interlude: theme in bass
    instruments

2:12 Variation

3:01 Interlude: theme in bass
    instruments

Track 3:
Menuet and Trios

Menuet: AB form, F major

0:00 Menuet: theme

0:33 Theme in dominant

1:06 Trio I: theme, D minor

1:27 Theme: A major

1:54 Theme: A major: return

2:23 Menuet: same as above

2:56 Trio II: theme, F major

3:24 Theme in dominant

3:52 Menuet: same as above

Track 4:
0:00 Theme

0:33 Entrance of violin soloist

1:00 Violin and horn soloists
    together

1:44 Violin and oboe soloists
    together

2:31 Two violins together

3:11 Violin soloist with orchestra

3:23 Violin and horn soloists
    together

3:43 Theme: return

Tracks 9 - 11:

Brandenburg No. 6 in B flat

Track 9:

Allegro

0:00 First theme: violas

0:49 Second theme (variation of first theme): orchestra

1:13 First theme (partial): F major

1:36 Second theme: dominant

2:16 First theme (partial): C minor

2:46 Second theme: D minor

3:35 First theme (partial): G minor

4:14 First theme (partial): E flat major

4:33 Second theme: development

5:05 Second theme: return

5:39 First theme: return

Track 10:

Adagio

Fugue over ground bass

0:03 First entrance: E flat major

0:21 Second entrance: answer

0:50 First entrance: dominant

1:04 Second entrance: answer in tonic

1:34 First entrance: C minor

1:53 Second entrance: answer in F minor

2:22 First entrance (return)

2:41 Second entrance: entrance A flat major

3:51 First entrance: G minor

4:48 Cadence in relative minor

Track 11:

Allegro

0:00 First theme

0:24 Second theme (alternates with first)

1:08 Third theme

1:56 First theme: return

2:20 Fourth theme

3:23 First theme: return

4:30 Third theme: return

5:17 First theme: return

4 ***Violin Concertos in A Minor,*** (BWV 1041), and ***E,*** (BWV 1042); ***Concerto in D Minor for Two Violins,*** (BWV 1043). Jaap Schroeder and Christopher Hirons, violins, with Christopher Hogwood conducting the Academy of Ancient Music. L'Oiseau-Lyre 400 080-2.

The court orchestra at Cöthen clearly boasted some splendid soloists, as is proved by the concertos Bach composed there from 1717 to 1723. It was also during those years that Bach expressed his delight in studying concertos from the Italian masters (above all Vivaldi) that had made their way north. Such music as the slow movement of these three concertos pays adequate homage to the way the Italians had made string instruments into sweet singers of eloquent if wordless melodies.

Although only these concertos survive, chances are that Bach composed profusely for his Cöthen soloists; the lost works cast their shadows in the form of later reworkings as keyboard concertos. (These three concertos also showed up at Leipzig, transmogrified into works for harpsichord.)

The D-minor concerto for two violins is, by some distance, the expressive masterpiece of the three. The "conversation" between the two soloists is the kind of writing Mozart later explored; the slow movement should be played for those who insist Bach's music has no soul. George Balanchine choreographed this music as *Concerto Barocco,* adding to it another measure of expressivity.

Tracks 1-3:

Violin Concerto in A minor

Track 1:

Allegro

0:00 Ritornello 1: opening

0:32 Solo 1

0:52 Ritornello 2 (under solo)

0:57 Solo 2

1:09 Sequence

1:21 Solo 3

1:24 Ritornello 3

1:26 Solo 4

1:29 Ritornello 4

1:37 Solo 5

1:44 Ritornello 5: (under solo) cadence

1:53 Solo 6 (with sequence resembling solo 1)

2:16 Ritornello 6

2:21 Sequence

2:45 Ritornello 7 (cadence)

2:50 Solo 7: motives from solo 3 and solo 2 in sequence

3:11 Ritornello 8 (cadence)

3:19 Solo 8

3:21 Sequence/cadence (fragments of ritornello); recapitulation

3:42 Tutti to end

Track 2:

Andante

0:00 Ritornello 1 (full): opening

0:24 Solo 1

0:37 Ritornello 2 (partial)

0:50 Solo 2: development with sequence

1:02 Ritornello 3 (with solo 2 sequence) (partial)

1:16 Transition to ritornello 4

1:29 Ritornello 4 (full)

1:42 Solo 3 (minor)

2:08 Ritornello 5 (minor) (partial)

2:21 Solo 4

2:34 Ritornello 6 (with solo 4 sequence) (partial)

2:48 Transition to ritornello 7

3:02 Ritornello 7 (partial)

3:12 Solo 5 and ritornello 8 (solo 5: transition material over partial ritornello)

3:29 Ritornello 9 (partial)

3:54 Ritornello 10 (partial)

4:07 Solo 6

4:34 Ritornello 11 (complete)

4:44 Solo 7 (last solo closing with ritornello 11)

Track 3:
Allegro assai

0:00 Ritornello 1 (full)

0:38 Solo 1

1:06 Ritornello 2

1:11 Solo 2

1:34 Ritornello 3 (under solo 2) with sequence

1:49 Tutti sequence continues with transition to solo cadence

2:19 Solo cadence

2:27 Ritornello 4

2:33 Solo 3

2:50 Sequence with fragments of ritornello underneath

3:10 Ritornello 5 (complete)

Tracks 4-6:

Concerto No. 2 in E

Track 4:
Allegro

0:00 Ritornello 1

0:29 Solo 1

0:37 Ritornello 2

0:44 Solo 2

0:51 Ritornello 3

0:54 Solo 3

1:03 Ritornello 4 sequences with solo 3

1:30 Solo 4 and ritornello 5 (together)

2:18 Solo 5 (minor) with sequence

3:02 Ritornello 6 and solo 6: sequences of both

3:35 Sequence under fragment of ritornello

4:08 Solo 7

4:25 Ritornello 7 (fragment)

4:39 Solo 8 with fragments and extension to adagio

5:18 Adagio: transition back to allegro

5:33 Ritornello 8: allegro

6:02 Solo 9

6:10 Ritornello 9

6:17 Solo 10

6:25 Ritornello 10

6:27 Solo 11

6:37 Ritornello 11 with solo 11

7:03 Ritornello 12 and solo 12 to end

Adagio

0:00 Ritornello 1

0:35 Solo 1

0:58 Ritornello 2 with solo 1

1:23 Sequence of solo 1: transition to minor

2:11 Solo 2

2:42 Solo 3: Transition to major

3:06 Ritornello fragment as shift to minor

3:44 Solo 4 with ritornello 3

4:07 Ritornello 4: full return with solo

5:02 Ritornello 5 to end

Allegro assai

0:00 Ritornello 1

0:17 Solo 1

0:34 Ritornello 2

0:51 Solo 2

1:08 Ritornello 3

1:25 Solo 3

1:43 Ritornello 4

2:00 Solo 4

2:36 Ritornello 5 (complete) to end

Tracks 7-9:

Concerto for Two Violins in D minor

Vivace

0:00 Ritornello 1

0:10 Entrance of both soloists: sequence on ritornello 1

0:53 Solo 1: violin 1

1:04 Solo 1: violin 2 with violin 1

1:35 Violin 2 alone

1:45 Violin 2 with violin 1

1:55 Ritornello 2

2:04 Solo 2 (violins 1 and 2 together)

2:18 Ritornello 3 (with soloists)

2:27 Solo 3 (violins 1 and 2 together)

2:39 Sequence

3:15 Violin 1 alone (original opening)

3:25 Violin 1 with violin 2

3:35 Ritornello 4 to end

Track 8:

Largo ma non tanto

0:00 Ritornello 1: continuous throughout; opens with solo 1 of violin 2

0:16 Solo 1: violin 1

0:29 Sequence

1:11 Solo 2: violin 1

1:27 Solo 2: violin 2

1:39 Sequence

1:57 Solo 3: violins 1 and 2 together: Part 1

2:08 Solo 3: Part 2

2:41 Repeat: solo 3: Part 1

2:49 Repeat: solo 3: Part 2

3:43 Transition

4:00 Solo 4 (violin 2): minor

4:15 Solo 4 (violin 1): minor

4:35 Sequence: transition to major

5:20 Solo 5 (violin 2)

5:36 Solo 5 (violin 1)

5:49 Sequence to end

Track 9:

Allegro

0:00 Ritornello 1

0:37 Solo 1 (violin 1)

0:45 Solo 1 (violin 2)

0:50 Sequence

1:06 Ritornello 2: sequence with transition

1:26 Solo 2 (violin 1)

1:34 Solo 2 (violin 2)

1:39 Sequence with cadence similar to opening

2:10 Solo 3 (violins 1 and 2): sequence with ritornello fragments

2:54 Solo 4 (violin 2): original

3:01 Solo 4 (violin 1)

3:07 Sequence

3:43 Ritornello 3: sequence with transition

4:21 Final cadence: similar to opening

5 *Works for Keyboard: "Italian" Concerto,* (BWV 971); *Chromatic Fantasia and Fugue,* (BWV 903); *Overture "in the French Manner,"* (BWV 831); *Four Duets,* (BWV 802-5). Christophe Rousset, harpsichord. L'Oiseau-Lyre 433 054-2.

The four works in this splendid collection survey a remarkable expressive range. The *Chromatic Fantasia and Fugue* is the only one dating from Bach's pre-Leipzig years, and even this powerful work Bach revised later on. The *Italian Concerto* is just that, an attempt to boil down a possible Vivaldi concerto, with its interplay between the quiet music for soloist and the full orchestra, into a work for harpsichord alone, with a marvelously Vivaldian melody as its slow movement. The French overture is actually a suite of dance movements such as the French public particularly revered; notice also the dazzling range of harpsichord sonority, with "echo" effects and other witticisms. The *Chromatic Fantasia* takes its name from the harmonic convolutions throughout but especially in the fugue subject, which turns and twists through sharps and flats in an artful attempt to conceal its actual key. Eat your heart out, Schoenberg!

The *Four Duets* come from Volume 3 of the *Klavierübung,* the same collection that includes the great *Prelude and Fugue in E-flat.* Composed for organ but without any use of foot pedals, this work fares equally well on the harpsichord.

Tracks 1-3:

Italian Concerto

Track 1:
Allegro in F

Ritornello form

- 0:00 Ritornello theme and first thematic group
- 0:39 Second thematic group
- 1:09 Ritornello theme in dominant
- 1:36 Episode from first thematic group
- 1:57 Third thematic group
- 2:13 Ritornello theme in sub-dominant
- 2:47 Episode from second thematic group
- 2:59 Ritornello theme in tonic
- 3:08 Third thematic group: return
- 3:30 First thematic group: return

Track 2:
Andante in D minor

Aria in binary form

- 0:00 Part A: introduction of basso ostinato
- 0:18 Entrance of "soloist" (in right hand)

- 2:16 Part B
- 3:52 Coda

Track 3:
Presto in F

Ritornello form

- 0:00 Ritornello theme and first thematic group
- 0:29 Second thematic group
- 0:59 Ritornello theme in dominant
- 1:32 Third thematic group
- 1:54 Ritornello theme in sub-dominant
- 2:09 Ritornello theme in relative minor
- 2:51 Second thematic group: return
- 3:08 Ritornello theme and first thematic group (return)

Tracks 4-11:

French Overture

Track 4:
Overture

Ternary form (ABA)

- 0:00 Part A: "French Overture"
- 1:13 Repeat

2:26 Part B: fugue I: first entrance
2:29 Second entrance
2:35 Third entrance
2:39 Fourth entrance
2:42 Sequences with fugue I
3:09 Interlude
3:28 Fugue I: return
3:32 Second entrance: return
3:39 Sequences with fugue I
3:52 Interlude
4:17 Fugue II
4:21 Second entrance
4:24 Third entrance
4:28 Fourth entrance
4:42 Interlude
5:15 Sequences with fugue I
5:51 Part A: "French Overture": return

Track 5:
Courante in B minor

Binary form (AB)
0:00 Part A
0:36 Part A: repeat
1:12 Part B in dominant
1:48 Part B: repeat

Track 6:
Two Gavottes

Binary form (AB)
Gavotte I in B minor
0:00 Part A
0:12 Part A: repeat
0:22 Part B in D major
0:44 Part B: repeat
Gavotte II in D major
1:06 Part A
1:18 Part A: repeat
1:30 Part B: in dominant
1:52 Part B: repeat

Track 7:
Two Passepieds

Binary form (AB)
Passepied I in B minor
Rounded binary form
0:00 Part A
0:07 Part A: repeat
0:15 Part B: in B Major
0:29 Part A: return
0:36 Part B: repeat
0:50 Part A: return

Passepied II in B major
Binary form
0:58 Part A
1:06 Part A: repeat
1:13 Part B in dominant
1:28 Part B: repeat

Track 8:
Sarabande in B minor

Binary form (AB)
0:00 A theme I
0:11 Theme I inverted in left hand
0:46 A repeat
1:33 B theme II
1:46 Theme I inverted in left hand
2:01 Theme II: return
2:36 B Repeat

Track 9:
Two Bourrées

Binary form
Bourée I in B minor
0:00 Part A
0:14 Part A: repeat
0:27 Part B
0:41 Part B: repeat

Bourée II in B minor
0:54 Part A
1:09 Part A: repeat
1:22 Part B in F-sharp minor
1:32 Part A in D major
1:42 Part B: repeat

Track 10:
Gigue in B minor

Binary form (AB)
0:00 Part A
0:22 Part A: repeat
0:44 Part B
1:29 Part B: repeat

Track 11:
Echo in B minor

Binary form (AB)
0:00 Part A
0:41 Part A: repeat
1:22 Part B in D major
2:13 Part B: repeat

Tracks 12-15:

Four Duets

Track 12:
Duet in E minor

0:00 Theme

0:02 "Echo" theme ("echoes" first theme each time it is heard)

0:11 Theme in left hand in dominant

0:28 Theme in left hand in tonic

0:32 Theme in right hand in tonic

0:46 Theme in left hand in G major

0:57 Theme in right hand in D major

1:13 Theme in right hand in B minor

1:26 Theme in left hand in B minor

1:37 Theme in right hand in tonic

1:46 Theme in left hand in tonic

Track 13:
Duet in F

Rounded binary form (ABA)

0:00 A: theme I in right hand

0:07 Theme I in left hand

0:48 B: theme II in D minor

1:17 Stretto (on theme I)

1:43 Theme II in C minor

1:55 Themes I/II in F minor

2:15 Themes I/II in C minor

2:24 A: theme I

Track 14:
Duet in G

0:00 Theme in right hand

0:09 Theme in left hand in dominant

1:01 Theme in left hand in E minor

1:09 Theme in right hand in B minor

1:33 Theme in left hand in C major

1:49 Theme in left hand in tonic

2:25 Final entrance of theme in right hand

Track 15:
Duet in A minor

Canonic form

0:00 Theme I in left hand

0:18 Theme in right hand in dominant

0:37 Theme II in right hand

1:08 Theme I in right hand

1:24 Theme I in right hand in dominant

1:43 Theme II in left hand
2:22 Theme I in right hand in dominant
2:39 Theme II in left hand
3:14 Theme I in left hand

Tracks 16-17:

Chromatic Fantasy and Fugue

Track 16:

Chromatic Fantasy

Through-composed: an analytical roller-coaster ride through all keys! Sit back and enjoy!

Track 17:

Fugue in D minor

0:00 First entrance
0:15 Second entrance
0:31 Third entrance
1:09 Third entrance in dominant
1:39 Third entrance in tonic
2:00 Third entrance in A
2:04 Second entrance (stretto)
2:07 Second entrance in B minor
2:31 Second entrance in E minor
3:00 Second entrance in C minor
3:42 Second entrance in G minor
3:58 Second entrance in tonic
4:23 Second entrance in tonic

6 *Harpsichord Concertos: for Three Harpsichords in D Minor,* (BWV 1063), and *C,* (BWV 1064) plus an arrangement for three violins in D; for *Four Harpsichords in A Minor,* (BWV 1065); and Vivaldi's *Concerto for Four Violins in B Minor* (Hogwood transcription). Colin Tilney, Christophe Rousset, David Moroney, and Christopher Hogwood, harpsichords; Christopher Hogwood conducting Jaap Schroeder and violinists from the Academy of Ancient Music. L'Oiseau-Lyre 433 053-2

The customary estimate of Bach's music as the summing-up of a century of musical style is fairly accurate. Yet Bach can take credit for actually inventing one important kind of music: the concerto for a keyboard soloist with orchestra. By 1720, the world was awash in concertos, but they were works for solo winds or strings (or now and then a horn or trumpet), with the keyboard performer as support.

Bach had composed many works in that format, but conditions at his Collegium Musicum for the Telemann Society in Leipzig suggested the experiment of a solo keyboard as well. He had tried out the idea earlier, in his fifth *Brandenburg Concerto* from his time in Cöthen; then, in Leipzig, he set about to create a repertory of concertos for one to four harpsichords.

Tracing the origin of these works both amuses and frustrates, for Bach recycled his own music as well as works by others. One keyboard concerto, the work in A minor for four harpsichords, is a fanciful, sonorous reworking of a Vivaldi concerto for four violins, B minor,

Opus 3, No. 10. (Those who saw the wonderful Cocteau film *Les enfants terribles* may recognize the music—the Bach version, that is.)

Bach transcribed nearly all the other works from earlier concertos (for violin, oboe, or oboe d'amore). None of the original versions survive, so violinists and oboe players have had a fine time retrofitting the keyboard versions. For one case, that of the *C-major Concerto* for three harpsichords, no trace of a prior version has been found. This may, therefore, be the one totally original keyboard concerto of the group. Christopher Hogwood, however, has filled in history's gap by making his own putative arrangement, the three-violin concerto also in this collection.

Tracks 1-3:

Concerto for Three Violins in D major
(Hogwood transcription)

Track 1:
Allegro

0:00 Ritornello theme

0:36 First section

0:50 Second section

1:12 Ritornello theme: third section

1:43 Fugal exposition: first entrance

1:48 Second entrance

1:55 Third entrance

2:17 Ritornello theme (variation): fourth section

2:48 Ritornello theme (variation): first section: return

3:07 Second section: return

4:48 Ritornello theme: variation

5:18 Ritornello theme: final statement

Track 2:
Adagio

0:00 First theme (motive in continuo runs through entire movement)

0:24 Second theme

0:55 First theme: return

1:15 Second theme: variation

1:55 Third theme

2:34 First theme: variation

2:55 Fourth theme

3:22 Third theme: variation

5:00 First theme: final statement

Track 3:
Allegro

0:00 First theme

0:50 Second theme

1:36 First theme: return

1:48 Second theme: return

2:34 First theme: return

3:35 First theme: final statement

Tracks 4-6:

Concerto for Three Harpsichords in C

Track 4:
Allegro

0:00 Ritornello theme

0:35 First section

0:50 Second section

1:12 Ritornello theme: third section

1:45 Fugal exposition: first entrance

1:50 Second entrance

1:57 Third entrance

2:19 Ritornello theme (variation): fifth section

2:52 Ritornello theme (variation): first section: return

3:12 Second section: return

4:56 Ritornello theme: variation

5:28 Ritornello theme: final statement

Track 5:
Adagio

0:00 First theme (motive in continuo runs through entire movement)

0:21 Second theme

0:51 First theme: return

1:10 Second theme: variation

1:48 Third theme

2:26 First theme: variation

2:45 Fourth theme

3:13 Third theme: variation

4:45 First theme: final statement

Track 6:

Allegro

0:00	First theme
0:52	Second theme
1:41	First theme: return
1:53	Second theme: return
2:42	First theme: return
3:50	First theme: Final statement

Tracks 7-9:

Concerto for Three Harpsichords in D minor

Track 7:

Allegro

0:00	Ritornello theme
0:40	First section
1:15	Second section
1:43	Ritornello theme: return
2:01	Ritornello theme (variation): third section
2:34	Ritornello theme: return
2:59	Fourth section
3:27	Fifth section
3:58	Ritornello theme: partial
4:21	Ritornello theme: final statement

Track 8:

Alla siciliana

0:00	First theme
0:24	Second theme
0:52	Third theme (based on first theme)
1:19	Third theme: variation
2:09	Second theme: variation
3:33	Drive to finish: with harpsichord flourish

Track 9:

Allegro

0:00	Ritornello theme: fugue: first entrance
0:04	Second entrance
0:16	Third entrance
0:20	Fourth entrance
1:56	First entrance (variation in canonic form)
3:12	First entrance (variation in canonic form)
4:06	Ritornello theme: final statement

Tracks 10-12:

Concerto for Four Violins in B minor, Op. 3, No. 10

Track 10:
Allegro

- 0:00 First theme: soloists and orchestra
- 0:16 First solo entrance: violin III
- 0:41 All four soloists
- 1:24 Extended solo: violin II
- 2:01 Extended solo: violin I
- 2:29 First theme: all four soloists alternate
- 3:19 First theme: final statement: orchestra

Track 11:
Largo

ABA form
- 0:00 A: Theme: soloists and orchestra alternate
- 0:46 B: Larghetto
- 1:38 A: (variation)

Track 12:
Allegro

- 0:00 Ritornello theme: orchestra
- 0:33 First solo entrance: violin I

- 1:02 All four soloists alternate and overlap solo passages
- 1:22 Ritornello theme (variation): orchestra
- 1:37 All four soloists alternate and overlap solo passages
- 2:02 All four solos alternate (but do not overlap) solo passages
- 2:56 Ritornello theme: final statement: orchestra

Tracks 13-15:

Concerto for Four Harpsichords in A minor
(Bach "transcription" of Vivaldi Op. 3, No. 10, Tracks 10-12)

Track 13:
Allegro

- 0:00 First theme: soloists and orchestra
- 0:17 First solo entrance: harpsichord I
- 0:43 All four soloists
- 1:27 Extended solo: harpsichord II
- 2:07 Extended solo: harpsichord I
- 1:18 First theme: orchestra

2:36 First theme: all four soloists alternate

3:31 First theme: final statement: orchestra

Track 14:
Largo

ABA form

0:00 A: theme: soloists and orchestra alternate

0:45 B: larghetto

1:46 A: variation

Track 15:
Allegro

0:00 Ritornello theme: orchestra

0:31 First solo entrance: harpsichord I

0:59 All four soloists alternate and overlap solo passages

1:18 Ritornello theme (variation): orchestra

1:32 All four soloists alternate and overlap solo passages

1:57 All four solos alternate (but do not overlap) solo passages

2:52 Ritornello theme: final statement: orchestra

7 ***The Goldberg Variations,*** (BWV 988); Andras Schiff, piano. London 417 116-2.

A certain Count Carl von Keyserlingk, so the story goes, suffered from bouts of neuralgia that robbed him of sleep. He commissioned Bach to compose an extended work for Johann Gottlieb Goldberg, a brilliant young harpsichordist who von Keyserlingk had in his hire, to play so as to put him to sleep. Instead of a set of lullabies, however, Bach created one of the most stupendous works ever composed for a single instrument.

From a simple made-up tune in the rhythm of a slow dance—but full of **ornaments**—Bach derived the outline for 30 variations that explored every feasible nuance of the tune, and added a few that were inconceivable. Not merely a string of successive variants, the work took on a distinct form: every third variation was a **canon** (and the interval at which Bach composed the canon grew progressively wider), while the free-form variations strayed further from the original theme but then dizzily circled back toward simplicity. For the last variation, Bach took two popular songs—titled "It is So Long Since I've Been at Your House" and "Cabbages and Turnips Have Driven Me Away"—and squashed them simultaneously onto the outline of his original melody; the original melody returns at the end, as the entire work retreats into silence.

Thanks to the extraordinary personality that the late pianist Glenn Gould brought to the *Goldbergs,* the work is now one of Bach's best-known extended works; Jerome Robbins even wrote a ballet to the music. In this performance performance Andras Schiff has worked out his own plan for when (and when not) to observe Bach's repeats, based on the subtlety of certain movements and the accessibility of others; Gould did the same. A note-exact, repeat-exact *Goldberg* might turn into a somewhat more tedious exercise.

Track 1:

Aria and Variations 1-5

0:00	Aria: phrase 1
0:27	Phrase 2
0:45	Repeat: phrases 1 and 2
1:47	Phrase 3
2:15	Phrase 4
2:43	Repeat: phrases 3 and 4
3:51	Variation I à 1 clavier (2-part invention): phrase 1
4:05	Phrase 2
4:19	Repeat: phrases 1 and 2
4:47	Phrase 3
5:02	Phrase 4
5:16	Repeat: phrases 3 and 4
5:45	Variation II: à 1 clavier (3-part invention): phrase 1
5:55	Phrase 2
6:05	Repeat: phrases 1 and 2
6:25	Phrase 3
6:35	Phrase 4
6:45	Repeat: phrases 3 and 4
7:07	Variation III: Canone all'Unisono à 1 clavier: phrase 1
7:21	Phrase 2
7:36	Repeat: phrases 1 and 2
8:07	Phrase 3
8:23	Phrase 4
8:38	Repeat: phrases 3 and 4
9:09	Variation IV à 1 clavier (passapied): phrase 1
9:17	Phrase 2
9:24	Repeat: phrases 1 and 2
9:40	Phrase 3
9:48	Phrase 4

9:55 Repeat: phrases 3 and 4

10:13 Variation V: à 1 o vero 2 clavier (duet): phrase 1

10:23 Phrase 2

10:34 Repeat: phrases 1 and 2

10:55 Phrase 3

11:05 Phrase 4

11:16 Repeat: phrases 3 and 4

Track 2:
Variations 6-10

0:00 Variation VI: Canone alla Seconda: à 1 clavier (courante): phrase 1

0:08 Phrase 2

0:18 Repeat: phrases 1 and 2

0:37 Phrase 3

0:47 Phrase 4

0:56 Repeat: phrases 3 and 4

1:17 Variation VII: à 1 o vero 2 clavier (duet): phrase 1

1:29 Phrase 2

1:42 Repeat: phrases 1 and 2 (pianist takes it up an octave)

2:06 Phrase 3

2:19 Phrase 4

2:32 Repeat: phrases 3 and 4 (pianist takes it up an octave)

3:00 Variation VIII: à 2 clavier: phrase 1

3:12 Phrase 2

3:24 Repeat: phrases 1 and 2

3:48 Phrase 3

4:01 Phrase 4

4:14 Repeat: phrases 3 and 4

4:41 Variation IX: Canone alla Terza à 1 Clavier: phrase 1

4:51 Phrase 2

5:01 Repeat: phrases 1 and 2

5:22 Phrase 3

5:31 Phrase 4

5:42 Repeat: phrases 3 and 4

6:03 Variation X: Fughetta à 1 Clavier (3 voices): first entrance: phrase 1 (bass)

6:08 Second entrance (tenor)

6:14 Third entrance (soprano): phrase 2

6:24 Repeat: phrases 1 and 2

6:45 Phrase 3: first entrance (soprano)

6:50 Second entrance (alto)

6:55 Phrase 4: third entrance (bass)

7:05 Repeat: phrases 3 and 4

Track 3:

Variations 11-15

0:00 Variation XI: à 2 clavier (duet): phrase 1a

0:07 Phrase 1b

0:14 Phrase 2a

0:21 Phrase 2b

0:28 Repeat: phrases 1 and 2

0:58 Phrase 3a

1:05 Phrase 3b

1:12 Phrase 4a

1:19 Phrase 4b

1:26 Repeat: phrases 3 and 4

1:58 Variation XII: Canone alla Quarta à 1 clavier: phrase 1

2:12 Phrase 2

2:26 Repeat: phrases 1 and 2

2:55 Phrase 3

3:10 Phrase 4

3:25 Repeat: phrases 3 and 4

3:58 Variation XIII: à 2 clavier (sarabande): phrase 1

4:24 Phrase 2

4:54 Repeat: phrases 1 and 2

5:54 Phrase 3

6:24 Phrase 4

6:57 Repeat: phrases 3 and 4

8:04 Variation XIV: à 2 clavier (fantasia): phrase 1

8:18 Phrase 2

8:33 Repeat: phrases 1 and 2

9:02 Phrase 3

9:17 Phrase 4

9:32 Repeat: phrases 3 and 4

10:05 Variation XV (G minor): Canone alia Quinta à 1 clavier (allemande): phrase 1

10:29 Phrase 2

10:56 Repeat: phrases 1 and 2

11:51 Phrase 3

12:20 Phrase 4

12:51 Repeat: phrases 3 and 4

Track 4:

Variations 16-20

0:00 Variation XVI: Ouverture: à 1 clavier: phrase 1

0:25 Phrase 2

0:54 Repeat: phrases 1 and 2

1:48 Phrase 3

2:00 Phrase 4

2:13 Repeat: phrases 3 and 4

2:46 Variation XVII: à 2 clavier
(duet): phrase 1

3:00 Phrase 2

3:15 Repeat: phrases 1 and 2

3:44 Phrase 3

3:59 Phrase 4

4:14 Repeat: phrases 3 and 4

4:46 Variation XVIII: Canone alla
Sexta à 1 clavier: phrase 1

4:55 Phrase 2

5:06 Repeat: phrases 1 and 2

5:26 Phrase 3

5:37 Phrase 4

5:48 Repeat: phrases 3 and 4

6:12 Variation XIX: à 1 clavier:
phrase 1

6:22 Phrase 2

6:31 Repeat: phrases 1 and 2
(pianist takes it up an
octave)

6:49 Phrase 3

6:59 Phrase 4

7:08 Repeat: phrases 3 and 4
(pianist takes it up an
octave)

7:29 Variation XX: à 2 clavier:
phrase 1

7:41 Phrase 2

7:54 Repeat: phrases 1 and 2

8:20 Phrase 3

8:33 Phrase 4

8:48 Repeat: phrases 3 and 4

Track 5:
Variations 21-25

0:00 Variation XXI (G minor):
Canone alla Settima à 2
clavier: phrase 1

0:15 Phrase 2

0:31 Repeat: phrases 1 and 2

1:04 Phrase 3

1:20 Phrase 4

1:37 Repeat: phrases 3 and 4

2:14 Variation XXII: à 1 clavier
(gigue) alla breve: phrase 1

2:25 Phrase 2

2:37 Repeat: phrase l and 2

3:01 Phrase 3

3:13 Phrase 4

3:26 Repeat: phrases 3 and 4

4:06 Variation XXIII: à 2 clavier
(fantasia): phrase 1

4:21 Phrase 2

4:37 Repeat: phrases 1 and 2

5:08 Phrase 3

5:24 Phrase 4

5:40 Repeat: phrases 3 and 4

6:14 Variation XXIV: Canone
     all'Ottava à 1 clavier: phrase 1

6:29 Phrase 2

6:45 Repeat: phrases 1 and 2

7:18 Phrase 3

7:35 Phrase 4

7:53 Repeat: phrases 3 and 4

8:32 Variation XXV (G minor) à 2
     clavier: phrase 1a

8:53 Phrase 1b

9:17 Phrase 2

10:05 Repeat: phrases 1 and 2

11:50 Phrase 3a

12:14 Phrase 3b

12:40 Phrase 4

13:36 Repeat: phrases 3 and 4

Track 6:

Variations 26-30 and Aria da Capo

0:00 Variation XXVI à 2 clavier:
     phrase 1

0:15 Phrase 2

0:31 Repeat: phrases 1 and 2

1:03 Phrase 3

1:19 Phrase 4

1:33 Repeat: phrases 3 and 4

2:05 Variation XXVII: Canone alla
     Nona à 2 clavier: phrase 1

2:17 Phrase 2

2:30 Repeat: phrases 1 and 2

2:56 Phrase 3

3:08 Phrase 4

3:21 Repeat: phrases 3 and 4

3:49 Variation XXVIII: à 2 clavier
     (fantasia): phrase 1

4:08 Phrase 2

4:27 Repeat: phrases 1 and 2

5:07 Phrase 3

5:26 Phrase 4

5:47 Repeat: phrases 3 and 4

6:29 Variation XXIX: à 1 o vero 2
     clavier: phrase 1

6:44 Phrase 2

6:57 Repeat: phrases 1 and 2

7:25 Phrase 3

7:39 Phrase 4

7:52 Repeat: phrases 3 and 4

8:22 Variation XXX: Quodlibet à 1
      clavier: phrase 1

8:32 Phrase 2

8:42 Repeat: phrases 1 and 2

9:02 Phrase 3

9:12 Phrase 4

9:23 Repeat: phrases 3 and 4

10:07 Aria (repeat): phrase 1

10:31 Phrase 2

10:57 Repeat: phrases 1 and 2

11:50 Phrase 3

12:17 Phrase 4

12:44 Repeat: phrases 3 and 4

8 *Magnificat,* (BWV 243); *Cantata,* (BWV 51) *(Jauchzet Gott in allen Landen);* Nancy Argenta and Patrizia Kweller, sopranos, Charles Brett, alto, Anthony Rolfe Johnson, tenor, and David Thomas, bass (in the *Magnificat*); Emma Kirkby, soprano (in the *Cantata*); John Elliot Gardiner conducting the Monteverdi Choir and the English Baroque Soloists. Philips 411 458-2.

Trumpets resound through both these exultant works: "My soul doth magnify the Lord" and "Praise the Lord in all lands." The *Magnificat* was one of two major Latin works from Bach's pen; the other was, of course, the *B-minor Mass.* When first performed (Christmas 1723), the *Magnificat* had German chorale melodies interspersed between the Latin movements; the "pure" form dates from around 1731. It's a marvelous introduction to Bach's choral music: short, radiant movements in various forms, along with lovely word painting. (Note the plunging melodic line as God hurls the mighty from their high thrones; note the missing final note, as God sends the greedy away empty-handed.)

Jauchzet Gott, which also dates from around 1730, tells a lot about Bach's regard for the human voice. In several movements here it takes on the role of a second trumpet, equal in rank and importance to the first; it's almost as if the words play a secondary role to the abstract exaltation of the music.

Tracks 1-12:

Magnificat

Track 1:
Allegro: Chorus

0:00 First theme: orchestra: D

0:55 First theme: "Magnificat"

1:20 Text painting: "Magnificat"

1:33 Second theme: "Magnificat" B minor

1:45 First theme (partial return): "Magnificat"

2:15 First theme (variation): final statement in orchestra

Track 2:
Andante: Soprano aria

0:00 First theme: orchestra: D

0:18 First theme: alto: "Et exultavit"

0:29 First theme (return): "Et exultavit"

0:40 Text painting: "Et exultavit"

0:51 Second theme: "In deo"

1:22 First theme (variation): "Ex exultatvit" G major

1:55 First theme: final statement in orchestra

Track 3:
Adagio: Soprano aria

0:00 First theme: oboe d'amore

0:28 Second theme: soprano: "Quia respexit"

0:56 Second theme (return): "Quia respexit"

1:37 Third theme: "Ecce, ecce"

Track 4:
Allegro maestoso: Chorus

0:00 First theme: "Omnes" F sharp minor

0:22 First theme: "Omnes" A major

0:28 First theme (return): "Omnes"

0:46 Development: "Omnes"

0:56 First theme: final statement: all choral voices together

Track 5:
Moderato: Bass aria

0:00 First theme: continuo

0:15 First theme: bass: "Quia fecit"

0:28 First theme (return): "Quia fecit"

0:32 Text painting: "potens"

0:55 Second theme: "Et sanctum"

1:23 Third theme: "Quia"

1:41 First theme: final statement:
      continuo

Track 6:

Andante sostenuto: Alto/tenor duet

0:00 First theme: "Et misericordia"

0:20 First theme (first variation):
      "Et misericordia"

1:00 First theme (second variation):
      "Et misericordia"

1:19 Second theme: "Timentibus"

1:50 First theme (return): "Et
      misericordia"

2:10 Second theme (variation):
      "Timentibus"

2:58 First theme: final statement in
      orchestra

Track 7:

Allegro: Chorus

0:00 First theme: "Fecit potentiam"
      and text painting in all
      voices: "potentiam"

0:29 First theme (return): all voices
      together

1:02 Development (text painting):
      "Dispersit"

1:08 Adagio: "Mente cordis"

Track 8:

Allegro: Tenor aria

0:00 First theme: orchestra: F sharp
      minor

0:21 First theme: tenor: "Deposuit"

0:34 Text painting: "Et exultavit"

0:41 First theme: orchestra: A major

0:51 First theme (variation): voice

1:21 First theme: final statement in
      orchestra

Track 9:

Andantino: Alto aria

0:00 First theme: soli flutes: E major

0:28 First theme: alto: "Esurientes"

1:18 First theme: "Esurientes" A
      major

1:41 Text painting: "implevit"

1:55 First theme (partial return): "et
      divites"

2:14 First theme: final statement
      with soli flutes

Andante: Terzetto

0:00 First theme: trio: "Suscepit Israel" B minor

0:54 Second theme: "Recordatus" D

Allegro: Chorus

Fugue

0:00 Part I: first entrance: bass: "Sicut"

0:07 Tenor

0:14 Alto

0:20 Soprano

0:31 Second entrance: soprano

0:39 Alto

0:44 Tenor

0:49 Bass

0:55 Part II: all: "Abraham"

Maestoso: Chorus

0:00 First entrance: "Gloria"

0:05 Text painting: "Gloria"

0:31 Text painting: "Gloria"

0:49 Text painting: "Gloria"

1:27 Final allegro: first theme (track 1): orchestra: D major

1:32 First theme: chorus: "Sicut"

1:50 Final drive to finale: "Et in secula" D major

Tracks 13-17:

Jauchzet Gott in allen Landen

Soprano aria

ABA Da capo form

0:00 A: introduction: solo trumpet/orchestra

0:21 First theme: soprano: "Jauchzet"

0:45 Text painting: "Jauchzet"

1:15 First theme (return): trumpet/orchestra

1:34 B: first theme: "Was der"

1:55 Second theme: trumpet

2:03 Second theme: "Und wir"

2:46 A: first theme (partial repeat)

Accompanied recitative

0:00 First statement: "Wir beten"

0:32 Second statement: "Wir preisen"

0:44 Arioso: "Muss gleich"

Track 15:
Continuo aria

ABA Da capo form

0:00 A: introduction: continuo

0:11 First theme: "Höchster"

1:16 Ritornello: continuo

1:24 B: "So soll"

1:42 Text painting: "heissen"

2:04 "So soll" (return)

2:21 Text painting: "heissen"

2:55 A: repeatp   103   103

Track 16:
Chorale

0:00 Introduction: two solo violins and continuo

0:21 First entrance: chorale melody: "Sei lob"

0:58 Second entrance: "Der woll"

1:36 Third entrance: "Dass"

2:06 Fourth entrance: "Von Herzen"

2:32 Fifth entrance: "Ihm festiglich"

Track 17:
Final aria

0:00 First theme: soprano/trumpet: "Allelujah!"

0:42 Second theme: trumpet

0:46 Second theme: "Allelujah"

1:00 Text painting to end: "Allelujah!"

9 *Matthäus-Passion,* (BWV 244) *(Passion According to St. Matthew),* excerpts; Kiri Te Kanawa, soprano; Anne-Sophie van Otter, mezzo-soprano; Anthony Rolfe Johnson and Hans-Peter Blochwitz, tenors; Olaf Baer and Tom Krause, baritones, with Sir Georg Solti conducting the Chicago Symphony Orchestra and Chorus. London 425 691-2.

Settings of the tragedy of the *Passion* go far back in musical history; the best known before Bach's tremendous masterpiece was the work of Heinrich Schütz, set for chorus and soloists unaccompanied. A modern setting that has won great praise is the *Passio* by Estonian Arvo Pärt.

From the disputatious exchanges by the two choruses, with a third chorale forming an angelic arch above the others, Bach's harrowing drama speeds through the Last Supper, the Agony in the garden of Gethsemane, the trial and Crucifixion of Jesus, and the rending of the veil of the temple. A tenor sings the Evangelist's biblical text to a bare **continuo** accompaniment; the answering words of Jesus are clothed in a halo of string tone. Four soloists sing the arias that reflect and comment upon the action. A contralto, singing the Magdalen's plea for mercy and forgiveness ("Erbarme dich!"), breaks hearts with the poignant beauty of her music. The chorus offers further comment but also takes part in the drama. When asked by Pilate what fate should befall the captive Jesus, it is the chorus that yells "Let Him be crucified!"

This is inescapable, moving music, the ultimate testimonial to the timelessness of Bach's creations.

Track 1:

Kommt, ihr Tochter: chorus

- 0:04 First entrance: orchestra E minor
- 1:26 First entrance: chorus I: "Kommt"
- 2:16 First entrance: chorus II interjection: "Wen"
- 2:38 First entrance: chorus III chorale melody: "O Lamm": G
- 2:59 First entrance: all three choruses together
- 3:19 Interlude: orchestra
- 3:40 Second entrance: choruses I and II: "Sehet/Was": E minor
- 3:51 Second entrance: chorus III chorale: "allzeit"
- 4:32 Interlude: orchestra
- 4:58 Third entrance: choruses I and II (expanded): "Seht/wohin"
- 5:21 Third entrance: all three choruses

- 6:13 First entrance (partial return): choruses I and II: "Sehet": A minor/E minor
- 6:35 Finale: choruses I and II chorale entrance: "Erbarm"
- 7:23 Fourth entrance: choruses I and II (completely realized): "Töchter"

Track 2:

Wiewohl: accompanied recitative: soprano

- 0:00 "Wiewohl": E minor and sequence of keys to C

Track 3:

Ich will dir: soprano aria

ABA Da capo form

- 0:00 A: first theme: two oboes d'amore: G
- 0:17 First theme: "Ich will": soprano and oboes
- 0:35 Second theme: "Ich" sequence of keys
- 0:49 Text painting: "schenken"

1:07 First theme (return): oboes

1:23 B: First theme: "Ich will": E minor

1:53 Text painting: "Ich will reich"

2:15 A: repeat

O Schmerz: tenor accompanied recitative with chorus

0:00 First entrance: "O Schmerz"

0:16 First entrance: chorus chorale melody: "Was ist"

0:31 Second entrance: "Der Richter"

0:42 Second entrance: chorus: "Ach"

0:55 Third entrance: "Erleidet"

1:10 Third entrance (expanded): chorus: "Ich ach"

1:30 Final entrance: "Ach"

Ich will bei: tenor aria with chorus

ABA Da capo form

0:00 A: first entrance: oboe melody: C minor

0:38 First entrance: "Ich will"/chorale: "So schlafen"

1:01 Second entrance: same text

1:20 Text painting: "Wachen"

1:59 B: (based on elements of A section): "Meinen Tod"

2:40 Text painting: "Freuden"

2:49 Third entrance: chorus: "Drum muss"

3:37 A (slightly varied): repeat

So ist mein: soprano/alto duet with chorus

0:00 Part I: andante: first theme: instruments (partial canon): E minor

0:51 First theme (in canonic form): "So ist"

1:05 Chorus interjection: "Lasst ihn!"

1:26 Second theme (together): "Mond und Licht"

2:03 Chorus interjection: "Lasst ihn!"

2:23 Third theme (in canonic form): "Sie"

3:26 Part II: vivace: choruses I and II: "Sind Blitze"

3:54 Word painting: "Blitze"

4:03 Second entrance (in canonic form): "Eröffnet"

Track 7:
O Mensch: chorus

0:00 Introduction: orchestra: E major

1:13 First entrance: sopranos: chorale melody: "O Mensch"

1:44 Second entrance: "Darum": B major

2:32 First entrance (return): "Von einer"

2:53 Second entrance (return): "für uns"

4:01 Third entrance: "Den Toten"

5:23 Fourth entrance: "dass er"

6:23 Fifth entrance: "wohlan"

Track 8:
Erbarme dich: alto aria

ABA Modified da capo form

0:00 A: first theme: solo violin melody: B minor

1:02 First theme: "Erbarme dich"

2:36 Text painting: "Zähren" with violin

2:50 First theme (return): violin

3:19 B: (elements of A section present): "Schaue"

4:15 A: (modified da capo): "Erbarme dich"

5:57 First theme: final statement: violin

Track 9:
Bin ich gleich: chorale

ABA Modified da capo form

0:00 A: First verse: "Bin ich" F sharp minor/A major

0:17 Second verse: "Hat uns"

0:32 B: "Ich verleugt"

0:46 A: Repeat "Ist viel"

Track 10:
Er hat uns: soprano recitative

0:00 Melody over 2 oboes da caccia: sequence of keys: E minor to C major

Track 11:
Aus Liebe: soprano aria

ABA Da capo form (without continuo)

0:00 A: first theme: solo flute: E minor

0:44 First theme: "Aus Liebe"

1:22 Second theme: "von einer Sunde"

1:33   Second theme: solo flute

1:57   B: "Dass, dass"

2:31   A (abbreviated da capo): "Aus Liebe": sequence of keys

3:36   First theme: final statement in solo flute

Track 12:
O Haupt: chorale

0:00   First verse: "O Haupt"

0:17   Second verse: "O Haupt"

0:30   Third verse (modified): "O Haupt"

Track 13:
Ach, Golgatha: alto recitative

0:00   Melody with 2 oboes da caccia: sequence of keys beginning with and returning to A flat

Track 14:
Sehet, Jesus hat: alto aria with chorus

0:00   First theme: Two oboes

0:29   Second theme: "Sehet, Jesus hat"

1:02   Choral interjection: "Wohin"

1:43   Third theme: "Lebet"

2:13   Second theme: "Bleibet"

2:45   First theme: final statement with oboes

Track 15:
Am Abend: bass accompanied recitative

0:00   First theme: "Am Abend": G minor

1:20   Second theme: "Sein Leichnam": A flat to G minor

Track 16:
Mache dich: bass aria

ABA Da capo form

0:00   First theme: orchestra: B flat major

0:40   First theme: "Mache dich"

0:54   First theme (return): "Mache"

1:37   Text painting: "begraben"

2:18   First theme (return): orchestra

2:56   B: first theme: "Denn er"

3:50   Second theme: "Welt"

4:14   A: repeat

Track 17:

Nun ist der Herr: quartet accompanied recitative with chorus

- **0:00** First entrance: bass: "Nun"
- **0:22** Second entrance: tenor: "Die Muh"
- **0:49** Third entrance: alto: "O selige"
- **1:31** Fourth entrance: soprano: "Habt"

Track 18:

Wir setzen: final chorus

- **0:00** First theme: orchestra
- **0:33** First theme: "Wir setzen"
- **0:55** Second theme: "Ruhe sanfte"
- **1:43** First entrance (return): "Wir setzen"
- **2:05** First entrance (return): "Ruhe"
- **2:52** Third entrance: "Euer Grab"
- **4:29** First theme: repeat

10 ***Das musikalische Opfer,*** (BWV 1079) *(The Musical Offering)*; Iona Brown, Malcolm Latchem, and Roger Garland, violins; Stephen Shingles, viola; Denis Vigay, cello; William Bennett, flute; and Nicholas Kraemer, organ and harpsichord, with Sir Neville Marriner conducting the Academy of St. Martin-in-the-Fields. Philips 412 800-2. Note: This recording is part of a 2 CD set that also includes Bach's *Art of the Fugue.*

At the age of 62, Bach journeyed to Potsdam, outside Berlin, to visit his son Carl Philipp Emanuel and a new grandson. Philipp Emanuel worked for Frederick II ("The Great"), himself an excellent flutist and decent composer. Bach examined the newfangled pianofortes the King had collected, and reportedly saw no future in the instrument. He played organ for Frederick, and the monarch responded by inviting Bach to improvise on a theme of his own. This Bach did, evidently to Frederick's satisfaction. More than that, he carried the royal theme back to Leipzig, and there created an even longer treatment, a "musical offering" in which Frederick's charming, chromatically twisted theme went through even more metamorphoses.

Like the *Goldberg Variations* and other works of Bach's last years, the *Offering* is an amazing blend of speculation and expression. Yes, the aim is to put Frederick's theme through its paces, but the result is a serene, deliciously complex demonstration of hidden beauties revealed. Capping the work is an enormous six-voice **ricercar** (an earlier ancestor of the fugue), in which the original theme seems to stride through the centuries. Indeed it did; the young Anton von Webern recast this movement into a work of his own, proving that some of *his* musical theories could gain resonance through the hands of Bach.

Tracks 5-10:

Musical Offering

Track 5:

Ricercar 1

Fugue

- 0:00 First theme ("royal theme"): first entrance
- 0:22 Second entrance
- 0:48 Third entrance
- 1:05 First episode
- 1:18 Second episode
- 2:54 Second episode (return)
- 3:35 Third episode
- 4:03 Further entrances of fugue

Track 6:

Canon ("Perpetuus super thema regium")

- 0:00 Harpsichord in canon with a variation of "royal theme" in violin

Track 7:

Canon I à 2 ("Cancrians")

- 0:00 Each (of two) lines are forward and backward versions of each other
- 0:25 Repeat

Track 8:

Canon II ("Violini in unisono")

- 0:00 Two violins in canon with a variation of "royal theme" in cello
- 0:27 Repeat

Track 9:

Canon III à 2 ("Per motum contrarium")

- 0:00 Two violins in canon with a variation of "royal theme" in flute

Track 14:

Allegro

0:00 First theme: flute

0:15 First theme: violin

1:03 Second theme: violin and flute in imitation

1:40 Third theme

2:08 Third theme (variation): violin and flute exchange each other's lines

2:27 First theme (return): flute

2:37 First theme (return): violin

Track 15:

Canon à 2 ("Quaerendo invenietis")

0:00 Two instrumental lines in exact inversion of each other

0:27 Repeat

Track 16:

Canon à 4

0:00 Theme (version of "royal theme"): first entrance: violin I

0:22 Second entrance: violin II

0:46 Third entrance: violin III

1:09 Fourth entrance: cello

1:32 Fifth entrance: violin I

1:56 Sixth entrance: violin II

2:20 Seventh entrance: violin III

2:43 Eighth entrance: cello

3:06 Ninth entrance: violin I

3:30 Tenth entrance: violin II

Track 17:

Canon Perperes

0:00 Flute and violins lines are inversions of each other

0:44 Repeat (partial)

Track 18:

Canon IV à 2 ("Per augmentationem, contrario motu")

0:00 Violin and cello invert each other's lines

0:53 Repeat (augmented)

Track 19:

Fuga Canonica in Epidiapente

Fugue

0:00 Fugue subject ("royal theme"): middle voice

0:17 Second entrance: high voice

0:33 Episode

1:00 Third entrance: middle voice

1:16 Fourth entrance: high voice
1:31 Fifth entrance: low voice

Track 20:
Ricercar II à 6

Six-part fugue

0:00 Fugue subject ("royal theme"):
     first entrance
0:19 Second entrance
0:37 Third entrance
0:54 Fourth entrance
1:20 Fifth entrance

1:46 Sixth entrance
2:04 Episode
2:51 Canon
3:26 Seventh entrance (variation)
4:08 Eighth entrance (return)
4:26 Episode
4:42 Ninth entrance (return)
5:27 Episode
6:04 Tenth entrance
6:21 Episode
6:56 Final entrance

Glossary

o

Aria A solo vocal piece, usually one part of a work in many parts, in which musical form and verbal expression play equal roles—as opposed to in a recitative. The aria is usually laid out as follows: one theme, a contrasting theme, and then a return to the original theme, with the singer more elaborately supported by full orchestra.

Canon The generic term for a kind of music growing out of a tune (melody, theme, subject), which is presented successively by the several parts (voices) that make up the work's texture. Take the familiar *Frère Jacques* as a simple example; someone starts the tune, and then another person comes in with the same tune (in imitation). Then someone else joins the fray, and after everyone gets tired, the piece comes to an end. *Frère Jacques* is a canon at the unison, because every voice starts the tune on the same pitch. In more complex canons, successive voices enter with the same tune but at a different pitch. Thus, if the original tune starts on a C, and the next voice chimes in with the same tune but on a D (higher than C by the interval of a second), that's known as a canon at the second; from C to E would be a canon at the third, etc. In Bach's *Goldberg Variations,* every third variation is a canon at an increasingly wide interval—from canon at the unison to canon at the ninth, with other musical forms in the intervening variations: a marvelous blend of mathematical exactitude and artistic expressiveness. In Bach's *Musical Offering,* several of the movements Bach offered to the King of Prussia were canons whose exact configurations were described in the cryptic messages accompanying the pieces.

Cantata   Its simplest meaning is something sung (as opposed to sonata, something played, or toccata, something "touched," like a keyboard). More to the point, the Baroque cantata is a piece in several movements (aria, recitative, chorus, chorale) for a large or small number of performers. Sacred cantatas made up the crux of the Lutheran church service; secular cantatas could be about anything—including, in Bach's case, a cantata on the evil of drinking coffee. (See also **keyboard works** and **sonata.**)

Cantus firmus   A melodic theme or subject, usually designated for contrapuntal treatment.

Chaconne   A single movement, also known as **passacaglia**, in which the music flows continually forward but also follows a pattern over a single harmonic pattern (usually eight bars) that continually repeats. It is, thus, a subtle blend of obsession and freedom; two Bach works (the chaconne for violin solo and the organ passacaglia) rank among the astonishing inventions in his instrumental legacy. (See also **variations.**)

Chorale   The term Martin Luther and his followers applied to the collection of hymns specified to be sung at each day's religious observance; Bach based each of his sacred cantatas on the tune and text of that day's chorale. The term is likewise applied to an entire choral movement clearly based on a chorale melody, as in the fifth movement of *Ein feste Burg.*

Concerto   From "certare" (to strive) and "con" (with or against), a concerto is an instrumental composition, usually in several movements, that generally has some division of labor between a solo instrument—

or small group of instruments—and a larger group. Bach also wrote and arranged solo works for one instrument (harpsichord or organ) that he called concertos, but even these imply an ongoing conversation between big and small sounds. A concerto movement in Bach's time and on through the early nineteenth century typically included ritornello (a passage or more for the orchestra alone), cadenza (passages for the soloist alone, of a showy or improvisatory nature), and tutti (a variety of sections in which the soloist and orchestra—for "tutti" simply means "everybody"—engage in all kinds of enlightened, if wordless, conversation). A **concerto grosso** builds on the differences between small and large groups of instruments.

Continuo or **basso continuo** The lowest line in a vocal or instrumental composition in which a keyboard instrument (harpsichord or organ), usually joined by a low string or wind instrument, supports the entire harmonic basis for the composition. In Bach's time, the keyboard continuo player typically improvised fancifully

around the bare notes of the part. The continuo was phased out of composition and performance by the early nineteenth century.

Counterpoint or **polyphony** The ability to present several ideas simultaneously in such a way that the ear can pick them apart is the special property of music. Since its invention around 1000 A.D., counterpoint has challenged composers to create works of enormous contrapuntal complexity while following the rules of natural and pleasing harmony. A Renaissance motet, a Bach fugue, a vocal ensemble in a Mozart opera —all are counterpoint in action. Counterpoint and polyphony mean essentially the same thing, as do the derived adjectives contrapuntal and polyphonic.

Fantasia A free-form instrumental composition.

Fugue A specific kind of counterpoint in which a single idea (**subject**) entering over and over in the upper and lower registers (of a chorus, an orchestra, a keyboard) is played off against itself. In Bach's hands, the fugue became a complex form in which many elements might appear. After the exposition, in which the subject is presented in all parts—sometimes extended by a counter-subject—the counterpoint may be relaxed for an **episode** of a more melodic nature. Later, the fugal subject may be played more slowly (expansion) or more quickly (diminution) than before. In the climactic stretta, the subject appears in successive voices more rapidly than before, thus intensifying the work's momentum. One can measure Bach's greatness by the infinite variety of "treatments" he devised for his fugues.

Imitation   The generic term for the process by which a single melody is taken up by one voice after another, in a fugue as well as in the contrapuntal works of the Renaissance, both sacred and secular. (See also **canon, counterpoint,** and **fugue.**)

Keyboard instruments   These date back at least to the Middle Ages (those who have seen the film *Alexander Nevsky* will surely remember the horrid old German priest at his portable organ). Keyboard instruments that activate a string (by plucking or simply hitting it) date back to the sixteenth century: the virginals and clavichord for home use, the harpsichord (with its louder ranks of strings and registers) for grander settings. All were gradually replaced in public favor with the invention of the pianoforte—an instrument much exploited by Carl Philipp Emanuel and Johann Christian Bach but for which "Papa" Bach had little use. By Bach's time, the organ had reached a high state of development. The surviving documents in his hand (collected in *The Bach Reader*) trace his experiences with the organ at his various places of employment, and his passionate though usually fruitless efforts to repair or enhance the instruments.

Keyboard works   The hundreds of separate pieces Bach composed for organ and/or harpsichord bear a variety of names, some interchangeable (and some, in fact, supplied by nineteenth-century editors). Generally speaking, prelude and toccata refer to the first of a pair of pieces, followed by a fugue. Of the two terms, toccata is usually a virtuosic piece that dashes through several unrelated ideas and gives the impression of an improvisation. A prelude can be anything else; the forty-eight preludes of the *Well-Tempered Clavier* (each followed by a fugue) are a compendium of Baroque expressiveness—fast and slow, loud and soft.

Magnificat *Magnificat anima mea Dominum* are the first words of the hymn of praise—"My soul doth magnify the Lord"—sung by the pregnant Mary (in Luke I). Luther retained this text in the service of his new church, to be sung at vespers, and Bach's marvelous setting was one of his few Latin works.

Oboe d'amore A lower-voiced relative of the oboe with, therefore, a more "amorous" tone.

Oratorio Lengthy musical dramas, with the biblical text set as recitative for both solo singers and chorus, and meditative arias, some of heartbreaking intensity and sorrow, using newly created texts. (See also **Passion.**)

Orchestra In his 1607 opera, *L'Orfeo,* Claudio Monteverdi became the first to lay out a score assigning specific instruments to specific musical parts. The end of the seventeenth century saw orchestras—aggregations of string players, plus winds, brass, and occasional drums accompanied by a keyboard player—employed in the palaces of nobles and the churches and the municipalities throughout Europe. Composers such as the young Bach were hired to lead and write music for these ensembles. The orchestra expanded during the eighteenth century through improvements in instrumental design and the addition of more winds and brass. Bach had a small orchestra at his disposal as the Music Director of Leipzig, along with a smaller informal ensemble that presented concerts of secular works at Zimmermann's coffeehouse—the so-called Telemann Society, founded by Georg Philipp Telemann. Bach produced a fine repertory of concertos for its use, some of them reworkings of older works.

Organ A keyboard instrument that uses a bellows arrangement to transmit wind pressure to a set of pipes. (See also **keyboard instruments.**)

Ornaments Musical "doodles" added to emphasize a note's importance in the melodic line—for instance, a trill, a turn, or a grace note. (The dozens of ornamentations boast a staggering variety of names.) Baroque composers expected their performers to sense where additional ornamentation might enhance a melodic line, and so ornaments were seldom actually written out in advance. (One exception: the slow melody that serves as the basis of Bach's *Goldberg Variations,* for which Bach did provide a complete set.) Fortunately, many treatises exist from the period, spelling out the which and when of proper ornamental practice, so anyone today who wants to sound "authentic" can obtain solid support.

Partita See **suite.**

Passacaglia See **chaconne.**

Passion The musical setting of the Last Supper, the Betrayal, the Trial, and the Crucifixion of Jesus as told in the New Testament and designated for performance during Holy Week. Bach's two authenticated Passion settings fall into the category of oratorio. Think of them as unstaged **operas,** the closest Bach ever came to composing in that medium.

Recitative A vocal piece in which the continuity of the words outweighs the notion of form. The typical Bach recitative takes its rhythm from the flow of words, very lightly accompanied by the **continuo.**

Ricercar Any of various musical forms (typically keyboard of the sixteenth and seventeenth centuries) in either quasi-improvisatory toccata style or polyphonic fugal style.

Sonata Although literally, the name means "sounded" (i.e., played by instruments), by Bach's time it had come to mean an instrumental work in several contrasting movements (slow-fast-slow-fast) but united by being in the same or related keys. The sonata could be played by a single player or a small group—sonata for violin and/or cello with continuo, **trio sonata** for two solo instruments with continuo. Since the continuo itself was usually performed by two players, this can mean a trio sonata is actually played by four performers. At times like this, only cool heads prevail.

Suite or partita   The predominant multi-movement instrumental form of the Baroque, along with the sonata. While the sonata usually contains movements of an abstract nature (including, quite often, a final fugue), the suite usually contains movements based on dance forms and rhythms: the allemande and courante (moderate to lively), the sarabande (slow), an optional minuet or gavotte, and a concluding gigue (rambunctious).

Syncopation   A rhythmic feature, whereby the emphasis within a measure occurs on some beat other than the expected one. If you have a march rhythm, for example, in

which the expected emphasis is on *one*-two-three-four *one*-two-three-four, and the composer upsets that regularity with, say, one-*two*-three-four *one*-two-three-*four*, the rhythm has been subjected to syncopation and the passage is heard in threes rather than fours. The duet "Wie selig," the next-to-last movement of *Ein feste Burg*, has some subtle rhythmic shifts heard as syncopation; those who really want to be driven crazy by a fluid rhythmic system full of shifting accentuation should listen to the first movement of Beethoven's "Eroica" *Symphony*.

Toccata   From the Italian "toccare," which means to touch, as in a keyboard instrument. (See also **cantata** and **keyboard works.**)

Variations   Any kind of musical treatment in which a known quantity (a melody, stated at the outset) is subtly changed in subsequent appearances without becoming totally lost. The variation technique can appear in several ways. The *Ein feste Burg* cantata includes a series of variants on Luther's original melody in separate movements: elaborately transformed in movements 1, 2, and 5, and in its simplest, unaltered form in movement 8. In two other sets of variations, the great organ *Passacaglia in C Minor* and the chaconne for solo violin that ends the *D-minor Partita,* Bach builds a single extended movement on an eight-bar repeating harmonic pattern. The *Goldberg Variations,* on the other hand, consist of thirty separate movements, each built of the outline of a simple tune heard in its pristine form at the outset and again at the end, but with the sequence of variations so planned—through a constant increase in complexity—as to create the effect of a single structure. Both this work and its only near-rival (Beethoven's *Diabelli Variations*) use simple, even trivial tunes as their basis. (See also **chaconne.**)

Further Reading and Listening

o

General Histories

Bukofzer, Manfred. *Music in the Baroque Era*. New York: W.W. Norton, 1947.

Lang, Paul Henry. *Music in Western Civilization*. New York: W.W. Norton, 1941.

Schonberg, Harold. *Lives of the Great Composers*. New York: W.W. Norton, 1981.

Swafford, Jan. *The Vintage Guide to Classical Music*. New York: Vintage, 1992.

Writings on Bach

Geiringer, Karl. *Johann Sebastian Bach*. New York: Oxford University Press, 1966.

Mellers, Wilfred. *Bach and the Voice of God*. London: Oxford University Press, 1980.

Mendel, Arthur. *The Bach Reader.* Edited by Hans T. David. New York: W.W. Norton, 1966.

Schweitzer, Alfred. *Johann Sebastian Bach.* New York: Macmillan, 1966.

Terry, Sir Charles Stanford. *The Music of Bach: An Introduction.* New York: Dover, 1963.

Wolff, Christian. *Bach, Essays on his Life and Music.* Cambridge: Harvard University Press, 1991.

A Selective Bach Discography

Instrumental Music

The Well-Tempered Clavier. Played (and better than you might expect) by jazzman Keith Jarrett. ECM 78118-21362/21433; 2 volumes, 2 discs each.

Sonatas and Partitas for Violin Solo. Astonishing, inventive music played with love and gusto by Romanian violinist Sergiu Luca. Elektra/Nonesuch 73030-2; 2 discs.

Vocal Music

Mass in B Minor. Its majesty and deep emotion beautifully captured by Andrew Parrott, with a small chorus and an authentic-instrument orchestra. Angel-EMI ZDCB47292-2; 2 discs.

Cantatas Nos. 29, 50, 140. Three resplendent and varied examples of Bach's sacred style, conducted by German scholar/musician Helmuth Rilling. Hänssler 98857.

Cantatas Nos. 211, 212. The most famous of the secular works, including the droll *Coffee Cantata.* Sir Neville Marriner conducts, with Dietrich Fischer-Dieskau among the soloists. Philips 412862-2.

Christmas Oratorio. Six cantatas, by turns contemplative and triumphant, retell the story of the Nativity. Nikolaus Harnoncourt conducts an ensemble with authentic Bach-era instruments. Teldec 9031-77610-2; 2 discs.

Passion According to St. John. More mystical and inward than the dramatic *Passion According to St. Matthew* and, in its climactic moments, no less powerful. Philippe Herreweghe conducts an "authentic" performance. Harmonia Mundi 90-1264/65; 2 discs.

Miscellaneous

The Anna Magdalena Bach Notebook. A collection of songs and keyboard pieces designed by Bach to teach and amuse his hardworking and prolific second wife. Nicholas McGegan hosts a happy domestic gathering to perform these charmers in the proper informal manner. Harmonia Mundi 907042.

Jazz Sebastian Bach. The original Swingle Singers, remarkable for their accuracy as well as their spirit, turn some of Bach's keyboard pieces into lively exercises in scat singing, with a percussion backup. Sebastian would have flipped. Philips 824703-2

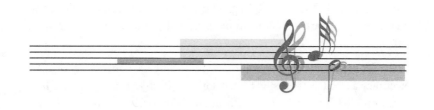